The Church Faces Death

The Church Faces Death

Ecclesiology in a Post-Modern Context

Michael Jinkins

New York   Oxford
Oxford University Press
1999

Oxford University Press

Oxford   New York
Athens   Auckland   Bangkok   Bogotá   Buenos Aires   Calcutta
Cape Town   Chennai   Dar es Salaam   Delhi   Florence   Hong Kong   Istanbul
Karachi   Kuala Lumpur   Madrid   Melbourne   Mexico City   Mumbai
Nairobi   Paris   São Paulo   Singapore   Taipei   Tokyo   Toronto   Warsaw

and associated companies in

Berlin   Ibadan

Published by Oxford University Press, Inc.
198 Madison Avenue, New York, New York 10016

Oxford is a registered trademark of Oxford University Press

Library of Congress Cataloging-in-Publication Data
Jinkins, Michael, 1953–
      The church faces death : ecclesiology in a post-modern context / Michael Jinkins.
         p.   cm.
      Includes bibliographical references and index.
      ISBN 0-19-512840-0
      1. Church.   I.   Title.
   BV600.2.J53   1999
   262— dc21   98-36522

Chapter 2 of this book was originally published in the *The Scottish Journal of Theology* as an article
titled "De-scribing Church: Ecclesiology in Semiotic Dialogue," and is reprinted with permission of
T & T Clark, Publishers, Edinburgh. Copyright © 1998. Excerpts from "The Blue Guide" and "The Great
Family of Man" from *Mythologies* by Roland Barthes, translated by Annette Lavers. Translation
copyright © 1972 by Jonathan Cape, Ltd. Reprinted by permission of Hill and Wang, a division of Farrar,
Straus & Giroux, Inc. Excerpts from Jacques Derrida, *The Gift of Death*, are reprinted with permission
of The University of Chicago Press, Copyright © 1995, tr. David Wills. Excerpts from *Open Letters* by
Václav Havel, trans., P. Wilson copyright © 1991 by Václav Havel and Paul Wilson. Reprinted by
permission of Alfred A. Knopf, Inc. Excerpts from Emmanuel Levinas, *The Levinas Reader*, are reprinted
with permission of Blackwell Publishers, Oxford, England. Copyright © 1989, ed. Sean Hand.

9 8 7 6 5 4 3 2 1

Printed in the United States of America
on acid-free paper

For
Jeremy Michael Jinkins
and
Jessica Michelle Jinkins

Depend upon it, Sir, when a man knows
he is to be hanged in a fortnight,
it concentrates his mind wonderfully.

Dr. Samuel Johnson
September 19, 1777
James Boswell's Life of Johnson

Acknowledgments

This book began as a response to questions raised by a group of ministers concerning the integrity and character of the Christian church. I responded to these questions in a paper (which in this book is roughly equivalent to chapter 5), but the questions raised were not fully answered. The problems certainly were not resolved. In particular, I could not escape the question, "What does it mean when we say 'church'?" In the introduction I shall explain my approach to dealing with this question. But from the outset I must acknowledge my indebtedness to conversation partners who in print and in the flesh have contributed to this work.

Anyone who knows James B. Torrance will recognize his influence on my interpretation of Dietrich Bonhoeffer, Karl Barth, and Eberhard Jüngel. I am also indebted to Colin Gunton, whose investigations into the meaning of relationality and the triune God have shaped my thinking in more ways than I am probably conscious. The influence of literary critical studies, theological hermeneutics, semiotic theory, and post-modernist philosophy are evident throughout these pages; the writings of Jacques Derrida, Roland Barthes, Michel Foucault, Umberto Eco, Emmanuel Levinas, Paul Ricoeur, Rebecca Chopp, Francis Watson, and Charles Wood have challenged theological discourse in profound ways, and this book reflects an ongoing interaction with their work.

My greatest debt, however, is to the community of scholars with whom I have the privilege of working on a daily basis at Austin Presbyterian Theological Seminary. I believe that our academic community at Austin is remarkable for its collegiality and esprit de corps, as well as the quality of theological conversation it gives rise to. I am grateful to busy colleagues who have taken the time and energy to read, reflect on, and critique these pages: Timothy Lincoln, Director of the Stitt Library, Stanley Robertson Hall, Associate Professor of Liturgics, Scott Black Johnston, Associate Professor of Homiletics, Stephen Breck Reid, Associate Professor of Old Testament, Lewis R. Donelson, Professor of New Testament, Cynthia Rigby, Assistant Professor of Theology, and Bill Greenway, Visiting Professor of Christian Studies. I am also in debt to the attention given this manuscript by George W. Stroup, Professor of Theology at Columbia Theological Seminary, Decatur, Georgia, and for the careful and tireless work of my research assistant, Carol Howard Merritt, and my secretary, Alison Riemersma. I want to express my gratitude to our seminary's President, Robert M. Shelton, our Academic Dean, Andrew J. Dearman, and our Board of Trustees who support our faculty in research and writing as well as in teaching. Finally, I wish to thank Iain Torrance, editor of the *Scottish Journal of Theology*, for his kind permission to publish as chapter 2 in this book the essay, "De-scribing Church: Ecclesiology in Semiotic Dialogue," which first appeared in volume 51, number 2 of that journal.

Contents

The Church Faces Death

Introduction

The cities of the New World have one characteristic in common:
that they pass from first youth to decrepitude with no intermediary
stage.

Claude Lévi-Strauss, Tristes Tropiques

ECCLESIOLOGY WITHOUT FOUNDATIONS

The point of departure for this study in ecclesiology is the anxiety in certain circles of the contemporary mainline Protestant churches, especially (though not exclusively) in North America, over their apparent demise. Within a comparatively short span of centuries, these communions, like New World cities of God, have passed from youth to decrepitude[1] and now stand astonished that they experienced so little of middle age. Their anxiety in the face of death is taken as a kind of complex sign, the significance of which this study interrogates as a way of gaining insight into what it means when we speak of "the church."

A generation ago a book on ecclesiology would have been a fairly predictable enterprise. Depending on the tradition from which it emerged it would have begun with biblical foundations, descriptions of the early Christian community (this generally would have been understood in a relatively homogeneous and singular manner as "community"), or a historical-doctrinal examination of the traditions and credal formulae regarding church. These foundational statements and descriptions would have been regarded as prescriptive for the life of contemporary churches in a kind of formula: Origin = Norm. The necessarily messy realities of plurality, diversity, particularity, and contingency that constitute the experience of actual communities of faith played a subordinate role in such approaches to ecclesiology. Center was assumed in a systematic approach that understood coherence as proof of truth. Foundations too. Such was the character of ecclesiology. Indeed, such ecclesiological assumptions are in evidence to this day, as we shall see.

This study begins in a rather different place, however. I cannot write the ecclesiology of a previous generation, nor would I be interested in doing so. Examining biblical witnesses to the early church, we do not find a single homogeneous or monolithic "community of faith." On the contrary, we find a polymorphic cloud of witnessing communities whose shapes change with the times and locales, the winds, and other atmospheric necessities, a plurality of communities in different contexts, bearing sacred traditions often at variance with other communities of faith. The Johannine community(ies), for example, gives expression to an ecclesiology that seems at points distant and foreign to the various and diverse Pauline communities and the Jerusalem community. If we are to take seriously the witness of the early communities of faith as a body of testimonies, a canon, we are compelled to recognize that particularity and plurality have been with the Christian faith from its beginning. Thus, for instance, to establish the shape and character of a first-century Pauline community (if such an endeavor is possible) does not establish the singular and non-negotiable norms for a community of faith in our own time—though we may understand more clearly how the gospel of Jesus Christ was heard and interpreted in the lives of the people in that particular community of faith, and we may understand more clearly in the process how we can hear and interpret the gospel in our own lives together. The lines of "application" between those distant contexts and our own are not necessarily straight lines; the light of illumination bends in response to the gravitational pull exerted by actual communities practicing Christian faith. We live through these communities of faith past and present; we form and are formed (and informed) by the interpretive, linguistic matrices of these communities as we conform to them, reform them, transform them, and sometimes transcend them. And so we examine our communities of faith through a variety of lenses that have been ground in the workshops of these same communities: readings of biblical texts, creeds, sacred stories, legends, myths, narratives, codes. All these textual relics contribute to the meaning-making in and among our communities of faith, but they do so best when we surrender our grip on them, when we learn to enjoy them and entreat them in the expectation that they speak not a dead *authorial* law but an authority that is liberated toward the communities that take them up in new contexts and in hearing them author them anew.[2]

This is play at work. And the anxiety of the contemporary western Protestant context works against such play. But how else can we raise so foolish and serious a notion that only in dying can we live? We have almost parodied the church to death. And nothing that can be said unambiguously can help us. Only paradox and its attendant play can save us from self-parody.

UNDERSTANDING THIS ANIMAL
WE CALL THE CHURCH

On Christmas Day A.D. 361, Gregory, the future saint of Nazianzus, found himself in the rather uncomfortable position of being pressed into ordination by his aged father. Gregory, as one nineteenth-century scholar wrote, was "stung almost to madness, as an ox by a gadfly."[3] Rather than taking up his pastoral duties in Nazianzus, he took flight to the monastic retreat of his friend Basil at Pontus where he hoped to escape what he described as the "noble tyranny" of his father and the church at Nazianzus.

Gregory did not remain long in retreat, however. Before Easter he returned to his father's side. He preached a homily on Easter, a sermon as remarkable for its brevity as for its profound and moving images. But he preached to a very scant crowd, especially considering the fact that it was the holiest day in the Christian year and prior to his flight to Pontus he was extremely well loved by this congregation. Gregory, aware of the displeasure of the people of Nazianzus, which their Easter absence made clear, prepared another sermon. Generally referred to as his Oration II, this sermon, which he never delivered orally, sets out his defense of his running away from the church after his ordination.[4]

In the course of discussing the difficulty of pastoral leadership, Gregory paints a vivid portrait of the diversity and complexity of the church, describing it as a kind of wild animal made up of many different animals.

> If anyone were to undertake to tame and train an animal of many forms and shapes, compounded of many animals of various sizes and degrees of tameness and wildness, his principal task, involving a considerable struggle, would be the government of so extraordinary and heterogeneous a nature, since each of the animals of which it is compounded would, according to its nature or habit, be differently affected with joy, pleasure or dislike, by the same words, or food, or stroking with the hand, or whistling, or other modes of treatment. And what must the master of such an animal do, but show himself manifold and various in his knowledge, and apply to each a treatment suitable for it, so as successfully to lead and preserve the beast?[5]

If one wants to understand this animal we call the church, one must take into account the fact that the church exists in irreducible plurality and particularity. Even if one only talks about a particular aspect of the church—the church in its congregational dimension as a particular local worshiping community, the church as hierarchy, or the contemporary Protestant church in North America or in Western Europe—one quickly discerns that the church possesses a complexity that defies easy answers and clear definitions.

This brief study in ecclesiology begins with the recognition that the church is so complex a beast that if we are to understand it we must approach it from several different directions at once. The book encourages the reader to participate in this exploration. None of the chapters intend to provide final answers to the questions they explore. Each chapter is an exercise in occasional theology, written in response to a particular issue in ecclesiology. Each chapter approaches the church using a different device. Each chapter asks the reader, "If we talk about the church in these terms, what do we notice that is not apparent when we talk about the church in other terms?"

The concern of this study is not to present a general introduction to the doctrine of ecclesiology. There are some good introductions already available, such as Edward Schillebeeckx, *The Church: The Human Study of God* and Eric G. Jay, *The*

Church: Its Changing Image through Twenty Centuries. These pages, by contrast, invite the reader to approach the subject of the church from various and sometimes surprising angles.

One might understand this book as a series of conversations occurring in different rooms. Each conversation takes place between the writer, the reader, and a number of stimulating, witty, and provocative texts. Some of the texts are concerned specifically with the church and the Christian faith. Others have no interest or only a passing interest in Christianity. From some chapters a clear and unambiguous argument emerges; other chapters offer only provocation and suggestion. Always in the background of these conversations, sometimes articulated, other times only tacitly, is death the issue, the question, the promise, and the threat—"the gift of death."

"CENTRAL" CONCERNS IN A DE-CENTERED ECCLESIOLOGY

While the chapters of a book unavoidably fall into a kind of sequential order, implying some sense of movement from topic to topic, the reader should be aware from the beginning that the chronology of the chapters in this book remains entirely arbitrary. One chapter does not necessarily build on another, but all of the chapters are necessary.

The Church Faces Death: Ecclesiology in Search of Identity and Responsibility

I shall begin by talking about death and how death raises for the church the crucial questions of identity and responsibility. The conversation begins with a recital of the familiar plight of mainline Protestant denominations in North America and Western Europe before moving into a close reading of Jacques Derrida's *The Gift of Death*.

Derrida, the contemporary French deconstructionist philosopher and directeur d'études at the Ecole des Hautes Etudes en Sciences Sociales in Paris, is one of the most compelling thinkers of our time. His *Gift of Death* engages a number of significant contemporary and classical texts (notably by Søren Kierkegaard, Jan Patöcka, Martin Heidegger, and Emmanuel Levinas), the Gospel according to Saint Mark, and some Pauline letters. This chapter lays claim to hope while rejecting optimism, affirming, with G. K. Chesterton, the church's unparalleled competence in dealing with its many "deaths" and the manner in which the church unconcerned about its survival is intrinsically attractive.

De-scribing Church: Ecclesiology in Semiotic Dialogue

Václav Havel, the writer and president of the Czech Republic, opens this conversation. For a few moments one may think that Havel carries on a monologue. But it will become apparent that the room is so jammed full of alternate texts that Tertullian and Dostoyevsky are forced to share a love seat. This chapter deals with the "problem" of images and imaging, of iconography, iconoclasm, and iconolatry, of tradition, faithfulness, and syncretism, of the relationship between the Word of God and the communities of faith that gather around and speak the Word.

Taxonomies: Paradox, Plurality, and the Enduring Genius of Church

The desire to classify persists wherever people try to understand what things are and how things function. The old joke goes that there are only two kinds of people in the world: those who think there are two kinds of people in the world and those who don't. This chapter recognizes the relative value of taxonomies and demonstrates their usefulness in ecclesiology by briefly presenting two of the most enduring ones, those of Avery Dulles and H. Richard Niebuhr. Taxonomies do have some serious weaknesses, however, and I shall also explore these. In the last section of the chapter, using what I call Hawking's principle of paradox (after Cambridge physicist Stephen Hawking), the reader is invited to reflect on how taxonomies can advance our thinking about the church by focusing our attention on those points where they do not work.

Speaking of Church: What Does It Mean When We Use the Word "Church"?

I draw attention in this chapter to something so ubiquitous that it frequently goes unnoticed: the language we use ordinarily in and about the church. This chapter consists of a reflection on ideas advanced by Roland Barthes, a leading French scholar in sociology and lexicology and a key figure in twentieth-century literary criticism, and Karl Barth, the Swiss Reformed theologian whose influence over theology in this century continues thirty years after his death. The chapter closes by asking the reader to consider what it might mean to think of church as a "sign."

Confessions: A Preface to Ecclesiology

Two questions Martin Luther King, Jr., asks in his "Letter from a Birmingham City Jail" provide the refrain of this chapter. Whereas the previous chapters use linguistic, semiotic, and taxonomical approaches to talk about the church, this chapter traverses the ground between an ethical and a christological approach in its attempt to discern what it means when we say "church." Also drawn into this conversation are John Calvin, Ludwig Wittgenstein, Edward Schillebeeckx, Paul Tillich, and Dietrich Bonhoeffer. In fact, Bonhoeffer provides us with the crucial clues as to how we can answer King's questions: "Who worships here?" and "Who is their God?"

Throughout the study a question remains: Is there life after death for the church? The answer is not obvious, but it is clear.

The Church Faces Death

Ecclesiology in Search of Identity and Responsibility

[K]eep death daily before your eyes.

The Rule of Saint Benedict, IV. 47

Set me as a seal upon your heart,
　　as a seal upon your arm;
for love is strong as death,
　　passion fierce as the grave.
Its flashes are flashes of fire,
　　a raging flame.
Many waters cannot quench love,
　　neither can floods drown it.
If one offered for love
　　all the wealth of his house,
　　it would be utterly scorned.

Song of Songs 8:6–7

Wᴴᴀᴛ ɪs ɪᴛ about the apprehension of death that is frightening? Are we simply afraid of the cessation of biological life, or of consciousness, or anxious because we are facing the unknown? Or is there even more to it—something in the occurrence of the apprehension itself that is an awakening, as from slumber, to the unavoidable and undeniable realization that we are facing death, that we are *alive-facing-death*, our death, and that we have it to face and to endure as a part of living? If this is so, if this is the nature and content of our apprehension of death, then is it not also possible that when the church as a human institution faces the prospect of its death, it faces its life, its *terminus* and its *telos;* it encounters an accounting for its raison d'etre and therefore its responsibility for its life and death, and the judgment of all that "church" stands for as a sign?

DECLINE IN MAINLINE PROTESTANT
CHURCHES AS A KIND OF DEATH

The headline reads: "Disappearing Church." The lead sentence: "The Church of Scotland will have no members left by the year 2047 if present trends continue, according to a new book by one of its prominent ministers."[1] According to Ian Bradley, author of *Marching to the Promised Land: Has the Church a Future?* membership in the Church of Scotland is declining by about twenty thousand per year.[2] With a current membership of less than eight hundred thousand, one doesn't have to be an MIT mathematician to figure out that the future looks grim for this Protestant body whose proud roots run deep into the sixteenth century and whose leaders have included John Knox, Andrew Melville, Robert Bruce, Norman Macleod, James S. Stewart, George MacLeod, the Baillie brothers John and Donald, and the Torrance brothers Thomas F. and James B., among many others.

Robin Hill, editor of *Life and Work,* the monthly magazine of the Church of Scotland, describes the church's steady loss of membership as its stroll toward a precipice. His criticism is leveled against the argument that the church's decline is merely a "slow and steady descent," as though it were a trend so gradual that it could easily be reversed. "If we want to be honest about the Church of Scotland's current membership patterns across the country," he writes, "then we have to undertake both a head count and a survey of the colour of hair on those heads." He reports that "more than 50 percent of folk in the Church of Scotland's pews are 45 years of age or older. Of these roughly half are of pensionable age. More disturbing is the census' suggestion that people in the 15–29 age range constitute a mere 8 percent of the Church as a whole."[3]

There are three other aspects to the decline in membership of the Church of Scotland: (1) the church's diminishing income, and the attendant problems of decreasing financial support for clerical personnel and reduced revenues for mission efforts and common ventures of the denomination at a national level;[4] (2) a significant lack of interest in, and frequently a suspicion of, the higher judicatories of the church—presbyteries and general assembly; a suspicion that emerges in the common references to these ecclesiastical bodies as "impersonal" and "bureaucratic";[5] and (3) the escalation in insecurity over, and internecine conflict concerning, the doctrinal content of the church's message and the relative positioning of parties: fundamentalist, evangelical, conservative, moderate, and liberal, especially as the church's teachings confront contemporary social issues.[6]

The anxiety occasioned by numerical decline and these attendant problems has led some in the church to a posture similar to that of the proverbial deer in the headlights—paralysis. Another common reaction, at the other extreme, is the hyperactivity of panic, which manifests itself in clutching for any and every programmatic solution and structural reorganization in the desperate hope that survival is just another project or organizational chart away. Neither paralysis, the desperate acquisition of innovative and frequently questionable recruiting techniques, nor a preoccupation with ecclesiastical administration make the church the kind of winsome presence in the world that leads those outside the church to say, "I will sell all I have and follow their God!" And, as Iain Paton has indicated, overindulgence in introspection and institutional survival does little more than distract us from the one thing on which our attention should be fixed: the gospel. His comments anticipate a possible response to declining church membership that is responsible and that bears further reflection. He writes: "The Gospel does not instruct us just to save ourselves: it instructs us to encourage the growth of the Kingdom of God throughout the entire world. If we simply look after ourselves then we shall be spiritually weakened."[7]

A statistical report from another branch of the Reformed family of churches, the Presbyterian Church (U.S.A.), parallels the uneven, but apparent, decline in active membership we observe in the Church of Scotland. Total active membership among this largest group of American Presbyterians in 1996 stood at 2,631,446: a goodly body of Reformed Christians. But this total represents an overall decline of 33,810 members from 1995. During the same period, the number of churches declined by 33; there are now 11,328 Presbyterian (U.S.A.) congregations. Infant baptisms declined by 1,315 over the prior year to a total of 39,060. The increases in this church are limited to two categories: The number of adult baptisms rose by 119 to 13,098, and the number of ministers increased by 143 to 20,783.[8] Membership in this church in 1995 stood at 2,665,276; the 1995 total represented a decline of 33,000 from 1994. Thus in two years the Presbyterian Church (U.S.A.) declined by over sixty-six thousand members. These annual losses were significantly less, however, than in 1994 when membership plummeted by forty-four thousand in a single year.[9]

Probably no religious body has studied more thoroughly its decline than the Presbyterian Church (U.S.A.), particularly through the seven-volume series *The Presbyterian Presence*, edited by Milton J. Coalter, John M. Mulder, and Louis B. Weeks.[10] The editors of this respected series place the loss of members in the Presbyterian Church (U.S.A.) in the larger context of the Protestant community in North America. Though their statistics are now over ten years old, they bear examination for the purposes of comparison: "Between 1965 and 1985, the United Presbyterian Church in the United States of America and the Presbyterian Church U.S. [the two denominations that united in 1983 to form the Presbyterian Church (U.S.A.)] together lost 28 percent of its membership." During the same period, "The American Baptists experienced a 37 percent loss; the Disciples of Christ, a 42 percent loss; the Episcopal Church, a 20 percent loss; the United Church of Christ, a 19 percent loss; and the United Methodist Church, a 17 percent loss. In all of these churches, the departure of members under age thirty accounts for the bulk of the losses."[11]

Many of the characteristics noted in the Church of Scotland are prominent among these North American Reformed communions: The church-going population is greying, attendance at worship on Sunday mornings is down, offering plates are lighter—especially when it comes to the undesignated giving that is crucial to the funding of the programs of the church beyond the doors of the local congregation (a trend that points toward distrust or, at least, apathy toward the church's work through what mainline ecclesiasts call "the connectional system")—doctrinal conflicts erupt along theological party lines, and social issues continue to bedevil attempts at functional and institutional unity.

Newsweek reported in 1993 that the Presbyterian Church (U.S.A.) slashed its budget by seven million dollars and eliminated 175 staff positions at the national level.[12] The preoccupation of this church, particularly at the national level, has centered on institutional survival, a fact that ironically works against its desire to bring numerical decline to a halt by attracting new members. Few people are attracted to a group whose recruiting efforts have the same emotional tone as that of a clinging, needy lover. One of this denomination's most astute missiological analysts, Darrell Guder, maintains that the church's survivalist tendencies provide neither a rationale nor an impetus toward the legitimate responsibility of the church to bear witness in its social context.[13]

In many respects, the United Methodist Church, the second largest Protestant denomination in North America, represents the most startling portrait of the apparent demise of a kind of Protestantism whose religious and social hegemony only a generation ago seemed virtually unassailable. *Christian Century*, arguably the unofficial voice of mainline North American Protestantism, reported a loss for the United Methodist Church of seventy-two thousand members in the United States and Puerto Rico in a single year, 1991. The decline in 1991 exceeded dramatically the stunning loss the previous year of 55,286 members.[14] Two years later the same journal explained that a denomination-wide program "to deal with declining membership is fraught with some of the same problems facing the church at large—a lack of money, charges of a lack of trust and wrangling among those involved." The article goes on to say: "The turmoil within Methodism is representative of what is happening throughout mainline Protestantism as it faces declining membership and revenues, suspicion of national bureaucracies, and controversial social issues—especially those linked to sexuality—that have led to conflicts within the denominations."[15]

A 1995 issue of the *Century* details another aspect of decline in this previously rock-solid, blue-chip denomination: "The average age of United Methodists continues to increase at a faster rate than that of the overall population of the U.S., according to a profile released late in May by the denomination's General Council on Ministries in Dayton, Ohio." The report explains that, according to Gallup polls, "40 percent of United Methodists were 50 years of age or older in 1957," that is, in the halcyon days of North American Protestantism; "by 1986 . . . this proportion had grown to 49 percent," while in 1990 "the percentage increased to 56.6 percent." A poll conducted in 1994 showed that the percentage of Methodists fifty years and older had grown to 61.4 percent.[16]

The news from Britain, the cradle of Methodism, does not inspire optimism. The *Century* reported recently: "If present trends continue, the British Methodist Church could vanish from Great Britain early in the next century." Peter Barber, the Methodist connectional membership secretary in London, writes in the *Methodist Recorder* that membership over the past three years in that church "is down by 6.8 percent." As disturbing as that figure is, his other numbers are even more distressing: Attendance at worship is down by 9.6 percent, "and the number of young people under the age of 26 involved in the church" is "down by 19 percent." While the British Methodist Church has survived dreary forecasts in the past, the 1.2 million Methodists in Britain have cause for concern.[17]

In all these three cases—the Church of Scotland, the Presbyterian Church (U.S.A.), and the United Methodist Church—one discovers similar issues: greying congregations; declining numbers of baptisms; lack of confidence in denominational structures of leadership and general diminution of interest in mission and churchly ventures beyond the congregational level; hand-wringing over theological perspectives and their consistency (or inconsistency) with traditional and confessional identity; and persistent conflict over contemporary social issues. Decline has provoked a variety of theological-reflective responses, ranging from Stanley Hauerwas's acerbic comment, "God is killing mainline Protestantism in America, and we goddam well deserve it,"[18] to Loren Mead's more sanguine spin, "God is always calling us to be more than we have been."[19]

Some researchers in the fields of ecclesiology and missiology investigate the perplexity of Western European and North American church leaders at the steady decline in these contexts and the extraordinary growth in membership in places that were once "foreign mission fields," such as Korea.[20] Others attempt to inspire the ranks by calling for various and sundry fresh foci (i.e., emphasis on congregational aspects of ecclesial life, concentration in the *ressourcement* of contemporary praxis by emphasizing the historic confessional standards of the particular traditions, attention to theological diversity in a global context, interest in spirituality and in cultural pluralism) and new patterns of organization in the church, patterns that are less hierarchical and less dependent on models derived from the top-down corporate business structures that dominated America, especially in the 1940s–1960s.[21] Another researcher, who has studied the relationship between wealth and membership decline in the United Methodist Church, asserts that "[o]ne factor in the decreasing membership of the United Methodist Church is the unprecedented affluence following World War II." He draws attention to research that demonstrates that "unchurched Americans are disproportionately white, young, educated, male, and affluent."[22] Apparently it is still difficult for camels to get through the needle's eye.

The literature on the church's decline seems to be the only thing growing in North American Protestantism. And it is a literature riding the crest of a tidal wave of anxiety that threatens everything in its path.

The assumption behind this anxiety and the supposition that undergirds a large proportion of the literature is that if the church simply remained faithful (and this "faithfulness" is variously defined) it would not decline. This assumption comes naturally to the North American spirit of rationalism (a rationalism that looks for simple cause-effect relationships to explain phenomena) and entrepreneurship, an entrepreneurship that meshes well with North American evangelicalism, a movement that was itself shaped by religious revivalism and also by the bourgeois myths of self-improvement and of the independent "self-made" individual.

In recent years this entrepreneurship has provided for many North American Christians the most persuasive interpretive filter through which matters of evangelism are understood. Thus the church's growth or decline is frequently understood in terms of market forces and product appeal. A business, after all, is judged by how desirable its products are in its potential market. If a business does not give the customer what it wants (and I do mean that a customer is an "it" and not a he or a she; the impersonal pronoun often dominates commerce), then the business will attract fewer and fewer customers wishing to consume its commodities and the business will (what is the word?) FAIL. The conclusion we are left to draw is this: If the church is declining in membership it must be because it is not giving the customer what it wants; nobody's *buying* what the church is *selling*. The decline of the church's membership numbers, according to this interpretation, points to the church's failure; to turn this failure around we need to find out what religious commodities are in demand, and we must peddle them.[23]

This entrepreneurial model, again, is consistent with the consumer-oriented approach to viewing reality in North America. But this represents, in the final analysis, a reductionist approach to ecclesiogy that discounts perhaps the single most striking aspect of the long history of the church catholic—the church's preference for martyrs over entrepreneurs, its honoring of principle over profit, its praise of those who are faithful and its ambivalence toward those who are merely "successful."

There may well be some truth, however, in the consumerist critique of the church's decline in membership, though the analysis is grounded in a faulty assumption and an inadequate conception of Christian axiology and ecclesiology. The truth in this critique can be stated simply: If people do not connect, for whatever reason, with the mission and message of a particular church, they are unlikely to affiliate with it; if fewer and fewer people connect and affiliate with its message and community over a period of time, a church will decrease in membership as the ravages of circumstance and actuarial tables eat away at the congregational rolls. But many reasons exists for the fact of declining membership—I shall allude to some of them later—and only the Lord of the harvest is equipped to discriminate between the faithful and unfaithful factors in church decline.

The point I want to focus on now is this: When the church faces the prospect of its own demise (for whatever reasons), it faces a critical moment when its vocation is called into question, when it has the unparalleled opportunity to comprehend and to render its life. When the church faces death, in point of fact, it encounters a critical moment when it may know the power of resurrection. But the church can only know this power in actually facing its death. Resurrection is not an abstraction, or a mere possibility; resurrection is impossibility, that is, it cannot be counted on in the normal course of events. It is not a guarantee. It lies on the other side of that which cannot be known. Nothing can remove the risk implicit in death. Full stop.

Jan Patŏcka writes, however, that "(eternal) life is born from this event of looking death in the face."[24] I would maintain that *this critical moment*—as Protestant churches in North America and Western Europe confront the real possibility of a kind of death—*is a divine gift,* a moment of crisis to be sure, but a crisis that calls our raison d'etre into question in ways that we cannot afford to ignore simply because the situation raises our anxiety. This facing of death can occasion a profound reformation of the church, which we have not yet begun adequately to explore; until now our anxiety has produced little more than a careening between the paralysis of our leadership and our frantic reshuffling of the same old institutional objectives and structures.

Only by letting go of our grasp on institutional survival can we possibly recover our vocation. "If any want to become my followers, let them deny themselves and take up their cross and follow me. For those who want to save their life will lose it, and those who lose their life for my sake, and for the sake of the gospel, will save it" (Mark 8:34–35, New Revised Standard Version [NRSV]). But to reflect on this possibility adequately we must take a detour.

Tout Autre Est Tout Autre

"Every other (one) is every (bit) other." So begins the final chapter of one of the most significant and theologically provocative books of our time, Jacques Derrida's *The Gift of Death.*[25] In this remarkable study Derrida reflects on what death tells us about human responsibility. His conversation ranges broadly from contemporary figures like Emmanuel Levinas and Jan Patŏcka to Martin Heidegger, Søren Kierkegaard, and Saint Paul. At the heart of his reflections there is the singular concern with the responsible human life.[26]

"[E]xistence excludes every possible substitution," he writes. Who I am is defined by a specific and particular context of social relationships that cannot be replicated. Each of us is constituted as an individual in the matrix of particular contextuality. Our singularity is as integrative being. To speak authentically of this state of affairs, one must speak in the first person singular, but with a profound sense of the otherness of others who share this contextuality.

I come to this awareness of myself for myself nowhere more certainly than when I face the reality of my own death: *I face my death.* In facing my death I face also the specificity and particularity of my life in relationship to others, which leads toward that point of mortal and moral singularity: *I am responsible.* As Derrida writes, "to have the experience of one's absolute singularity and apprehend one's own death, amounts to the same thing." While each of us faces death from within a particular social and historical matrix—which is also that which defines our human particularity (we are who we are by virtue of our contextuality)—each of us also faces our death as that which is singularly our own. Or, *I face my death as that which is singularly my own.* "Death is," Derrida continues, "very much that which nobody else can undergo or confront in my place. My irreplaceability is therefore conferred, delivered, 'given,' one can say, by death." Thus "It is from the site of death as the place of my irreplaceability, that is, of my singularity, that I feel called to responsibility. In this sense only a mortal can be responsible."[27]

For the Christian, Derrida's words are especially poignant because we bear witness to the gospel of Jesus Christ, the one in whom God is incarnate and through whom mortality is introduced into the being of the Immortal God. God in Jesus Christ assumes humanity to heal humanity, but, in so doing, this *end* that is peculiarly the creaturely end enters into God, and so we now may speak of God not only as free but as responsible.

"Then he [Jesus] began to teach them that the Son of Man must undergo great suffering, and be rejected by the elders, the chief priests, and the scribes, and be killed, and after three days rise again. He said this quite openly." But notice the reaction of Jesus' disciple, Simon Peter. "And Peter took him aside and began to rebuke him." Why? What is happening here? Jesus introduces death into the mission of the messiah.[28] But listen to his rebuke of Peter. "But turning and looking at his disciples, he rebuked Peter and said, 'Get behind me, Satan! For you are setting your mind not on divine things but on human things.'" (Mark 8:31–33) Jesus implies that his taking on of this mission—and the death that is for Jesus inseparable from this mission—is a divine thing; this most human end is taken up, as it were, by the divine and is placed in opposition to that which is evil and weak, even demonic—but also humanly tempting.

Jesus, in the next words of the text, draws together his mission as messiah with the call to follow him. "He called the crowd with his disciples, and said to them, 'If any want [ei tis thelei, "if someone desires"] to become my followers [simply: opiso mou akolouthein, "to follow me"], let them deny themselves [aparnēsastho heuton, the same word used in Luke 22:61 for denial-betrayal: "The Lord turned and looked at Peter. Then Peter remembered the word of the Lord, how he had said to him, 'Before the cock crows today, you will deny (aparnēsē) me three times."] and take up their cross [kai apato ton stauron autou] and follow me [kai akoloutheito moi]. For those who want to save their life will lose it, and those who lose their life for my sake, and for the sake of the gospel, will save it" (Mark 8:34–35).

Jesus looks at Peter in rebuke, then looking away from Peter to the other disciples, he calls them to deny themselves (Mark 8); Jesus looks at Peter and Peter remembers that his denial of Jesus was foretold by Jesus (Luke 22). Denial, first, as putting aside one's own interests in order to follow the messiah—denial; denial, second, as betrayal, as putting one's interest in survival above one's loyalty to and love for the messiah; denial in both instances as a handing over to death—death as the triumph of messiah's opponents, and death as the crucible of discipleship—death as the metaphor for the paradox of redemption. "Hos gar ean thelē tēn psuchēn autou sosai apolesei autēn," "for whoever desires to save his life, he will lose it." "Hos d' an apolesei tēn psuchēn autou heneken emou kai tou euangeliou sosei autēn," "but whoever loses his life for my sake and the good news will save it." The rendering of our lives toward death as the loss of existence is the supreme test of existence as disciples, those called to follow the messiah. The disciple is one who looks death in the face.[29]

Vocation (calling) and responsibility are inseparable; and, inseparable as they are from one another, they are also and even more profoundly inseparable from death. *Moralité* is inextricably bound to *mort.*

Derrida comments on and through Martin Heidegger, and his comments play variations on the theme introduced by Patŏcka. In *Sein und Zeit,* Heidegger "passes from a chapter where he was dealing with Being-towards-death to a chapter on conscience (*Gewissen*), the call (*Ruf*), responsibility in the face of the call, and even responsibility as originary guilt (*Schuldigsein*). And he had indeed signaled that death is the place of one's irreplaceability."[30] "Calling," as Heidegger sees, "is a mode of *discourse.* The call of conscience has the character of an *appeal* to *Dasein* [Being] by calling it to its ownmost potentiality-for-Being-its-Self; and this is done by way of *summoning* it to its ownmost Being-guilty."[31] Our authentic apprehension of our death contains, as it were, the possibility for this call of the conscience to be heard as a summons to responsiblity, but responsibility negatively apprehended in the face of death as guilt.

For the Christian, however, this Being-towards-death, which in its inevitability might be viewed merely as an owning up to the accident of mortality, is embraced as offering (the sacrifice of the cross that *can only* be taken up; the choice to refuse the cross—and so to live in bondage to the law of death—is inherent in its being the cross). And the judgment it delivers upon the singularity of our human life is also embraced not only as a claim on our responsibility as a kind of righteousness of which we are capable (Being-guilty), but specifically as a claim on our responsibility *to follow* an-other/an-Other (who "is every [bit] the other") and to place ourselves at the disposal of his "other" righteousness. Therefore, while my death is mine and no one else can stand in my place, can die as substitute for me, nevertheless in Christian communities we believe we place our individual deaths in the hands of Christ in such a way that we are compelled to say that we die *in him* because he has died for us.

The Pauline author of Galatians writes: "For through the law I died to the law, so that I might live to God" [ego gar dia nomou nomo apethanon hina Theo zeso]. "I have been crucified with Christ; and it is no longer I who live, but it is Christ who lives in me" [Christo sunestauromai. Zo de ouketi ego, zē de en emoi Christos]

(Galatians 2:19 – 20). The radicality of this claim, taking up the cross of following Christ as a participation in the crucifixion of Christ, represents a displacement of self, a loss of self. (*I no longer am I. I no longer am. I am lost.*)[32] Thus the freedom to take up the cross is a freedom to live, but it is not freedom in the popular sense of a choice arbitrarily made from among a set of options, nor is it a freedom toward self-actualization, as a claiming of one's own life. The life toward God is a participation in the crucifixion of the Messiah, a participation in the Messiah who is crucified. This crucifixion in which we freely participate annuls the claim of the law—as the sign of responsibility as guilt—and releases the follower of Jesus to live toward God. "And the life I now live in the flesh [en sarki], I live by faith [en pistei] in the Son of God [huiou tou Theou], who loved me and gave himself for me [tou agapēsantos me kai paradontos heauton huper emou]" (Galatians 2:20b). This epistle, which Martin Luther called his spouse, espouses in the next passage that conception of re-sponsibility that for the Christian relativizes all other claims to goodness: "I do not nullify the grace of God; for if justification comes through law, then Christ died for nothing" (Galatians 2:21).

And so the death that calls us to responsibility in its recognition of our particu-larity also calls us to a responsibility through our own particularity that for the Christian belongs specifically and uniquely to Jesus Christ. We find in this facing of our death that Christ died for us and we die for Jesus. To witness is to martyr.[33] There is in the Christian conception of vocation and death, of discipleship and wit-ness and responsibility, a mutuality of substitution, a substitutionary at-onement between Jesus Christ and us, a "mirifica commutatio" (the "wonderful exchange" of patristic writers and John Calvin) that is grounded in the actuality of the incarna-tion and that continues to be played out existentially in the life of Christians.

Even the singularity of physical death is, therefore, not an act in isolation. We do not die alone. We die in and through communities of faith—and have antici-pated throughout the life of faith this death—because we have died and were cru-cified in the death and crucifixion of Jesus Christ. The community bears us in this death throughout our lives. Heidegger implies the presence of community in his assessment of call as discourse. We die in and through a community of discourse —*discourse always implies community*—which brings to death (!) all the resources of language; and for Christians this general fact of mortality takes on an extraordi-nary and altogether separate peculiarity because we die under the sign of the cross in and through *communio lectionis*, community of the words of the Word who pen-etrated death and, we believe, emerged from death speaking.

"Dying in Christ" and "risen in Christ" become the sacramental names given to our existence as followers of Jesus Christ. This is what Dietrich Bonhoeffer meant, at least in part, when he wrote of the cost of discipleship:

> To endure the cross is not a tragedy; it is the suffering which is the fruit of an
> exclusive allegiance to Jesus Christ. When it comes, it is not an accident, but a

necessity. It is not the sort of suffering which is inseparable from this mortal life, but the suffering which is an essential part of the specifically Christian life. It is not suffering *per se* but suffering-and-rejection, and not rejection for any cause or conviction of our own, but rejection for the sake of Christ. If our Christianity has ceased to be serious about discipleship, if we have watered down the gospel into emotional uplift which makes no costly demands and which fails to distinguish between natural and Christian existence, then we cannot help regarding the cross as an ordinary everyday calamity, as one of the trials and tribulations of life. We have then forgotten that the cross means rejection and shame as well as suffering. The Psalmist was lamenting that he was despised and rejected of men, and that is an essential quality of the suffering of the cross. But this notion has ceased to be intelligible to a Christianity which can no longer see any difference between an ordinary human life and a life committed to Christ. The cross means sharing the suffering of Christ to the last and to the fullest. . . . As we embark upon discipleship we surrender ourselves to Christ in union with his death—we give over our lives to death. Thus it [discipleship] begins; the cross is not the terrible end to an otherwise godfearing and happy life, but it meets us at the beginning of our communion with Christ. When Christ calls a man, he bids him come and die.[34]

The singularity of human life and the call to responsibility toward which every death points, as Derrida affirms, in concurrence with Heidegger, are deepened, yes; but, more, the singularity of human life and the call to responsibility toward which every death points are transformed, converted, for the Christian. The general and inevitable mortality passes through the baptismal purgation of another death. As Puritan writer John Owen affirmed, following Saint Paul, the death of Christ is the death of death. Therefore the responsibility toward which our death points is the responsibility to receive Christ's response in the face of death (even death on a cross) on our behalf. The author of the Epistle to the Ephesians speaks of us as already "dead in our trespasses," in the sum of all we commit and omit contrary to what is right; but dead as we are, God has "made us alive together with Christ—by grace you have been saved—and raised us up with him and seated us with him in the heavenly places in Christ Jesus" (Ephesians 2:4–6). Our embrace of the crucifixion of Christ consists in an exchange of our death in trespasses for this other death, which we believe is itself life—but only our life as we participate in the death/life of another, and are given this death/life by the other (who is every [bit] other).

Ephesians reiterates the reversal of the general conception of responsibility, removing the condemnation that lurks within the threat (or promise) of death as "Being-guilty." "For by grace you have been saved by faith, and this is not your own doing; it is the gift of God ("theou to doron")—not the result of works, so that no one may boast" (Ephesians 2:8). The life toward which an apprehension of death compels us consists in life thrown back on ourselves and our own resources, life-toward-death, death in our trespasses;[35] but the life toward which our contemplation of the death of Christ compels us is life-toward-the-death-of-an-other, life that has located itself in the death of Jesus Christ; and it is life that must be found in the death of Christ in the particularity and singularity of our own existence. The death we die we die in Christ; but this death is also the death we live originately out-of daily because it is not merely the end of biological life or consciousness as generally conceived, not even the life-toward-death that awakens conscience, it is the expression of a specifically Christian conscience, literally a knowledge we receive together with and from and through community of the Word of God, the formation of a *conscientia crucis* that alone calls us to deny ourselves for the sake of the other.

Returning to Derrida's reflection on Heidegger, we confront the problem of the impossibility of one death taking the place of another, a situation specifically problematic with reference to what we have already affirmed regarding the Christian understanding of *mirifica commutatio*.

> The sense of responsibility is in all cases defined as a mode of "giving oneself death." Once it is established that I cannot die *for* another (in his place) although I can die *for* him (by sacrificing myself for him or dying before his eyes), my own death becomes this irreplaceability that I must assume if I wish to have access to what is absolutely mine. My first and last responsibility, my first and last desire, is that responsibility of responsibility that relates me to what no one else can do in my place. It is thus also the very context of the *Eigentlichkeit* that, by caring, authentically relates me to my own possibility as possibility and freedom of the *Dasein*. The literality of this theme, that is essential to *Being and Time,* can be understood in its strictest sense as the irreplaceability of death.[36]

"Everyone," Derrida continues, in this vein, "must assume his own death, that is to say the one thing in the world that no one else can either give or take: therein resides freedom and responsibility."[37] But of what character is this freedom and responsibility? It is on the level of general human experience, we must conclude, a bondage toward this end: We must die; we must each and all go the way of all flesh. Our only freedom lies in relation to this inevitability: How shall I *live* toward this end? And our responsibility is tied inextricably to our particularity: How shall *I* live toward this end? How else can we say it? As Derrida writes, still in and through Heidegger: "The sameness of the self, what remains irreplaceable in dying, only becomes what it is, in the sense of an identity as a relation of the self to itself, by means of this idea of mortality as irreplaceability."[38] Again, as he says in a manner reminiscent of Kierkegaard's *Sickness unto Death*: "My first and last responsibility, my first and last desire, is that responsibility of responsibility that relates me to what no one else can do in my place."[39] All of this is quite simply true when we apprehend death as the inevitable end of human life.

But, again, this general conceptuality of Being-toward-death undergoes a baptismal purgation in the context of communities of the Word of God. The inevitability is here among us. The freedom of the act of embracing the inevitability is here. But there is in the freedom a handing over of freedom that is the mark of freedom for those who follow Christ, and it is precisely in this handing over of freedom in the act of vulnerability and limitation that the Christian is delivered from bondage to death.[40] It is signaled in a Johannine saying of Jesus: " 'Very truly, I tell you [the risen Jesus is said to speak to Peter] when you were younger you used to fasten your own belt and to go wherever you wished. But when you grow old, you will stretch out your hands, and someone else will fasten a belt around you and take you where you do not wish to go.' (He [Jesus] said this to indicate the kind of death by which he [Peter] would glorify God.) After this he [Jesus] said to him [Peter], 'Follow me' " (John 21:18–19).

It would appear that following Jesus means giving ourselves over to him in such a way as to invite a kind of death, a freedom consisting in the denial of being-free to do as we wish. Indeed, this appears to be the very essence (if one can use such a word) of freedom, a rendering of freedom as self-determination to the determination of the Other, the Christ, that entails a surrender of self-determination to the will of others who wish to do us injury, who "take our life." If this is the case, then, the Christian's assumption of responsibility is, itself, a letting go *in the name of Christ* of even this most basic human call (the call to responsibility).

Is the Christian's location of herself in Christ's death, therefore, a shirking of responsibility, a ducking of that identification of myself as myself in the radical and irreplaceable particularity of my own life-toward-death? Such has been the age-old controversy between antinomianism and law.

Saint Paul in the Epistle to the Romans announces: "There is therefore now no condemnation for those who are in Christ Jesus. For the law of the Spirit of life in Christ Jesus has set you free from the law of sin and of death" (Romans 8:1–2). From the earliest utterances of the Christian community it was recognized that consciousness of responsibility is grounded in consciousness of death. Saint Paul contends, however, that there is a deadly quality to the consciousness of responsibility that is merely grounded in the consciousness of our own death, that such a consciousness of responsibility does not give life but only perpetuates the consciousness of human guilt and failure in the face of the immutable *ought* conferred in the singularity of death. The announcement of freedom from condemnation in the Pauline texts is grounded, therefore, in our union with Christ Jesus, in Christ's death and life, a union that we do not effect by contemplation or reflection but that is given us by God through "the Spirit of God" who "dwells in you" (Romans 8:9). In Christ, therefore, I lose not only my life but the singularity of my death and the responsibility (and accompanying condemnation in the face of this responsibility) to which I could naturally lay claim. My freedom in the Spirit consists in the fact that all I have is lost; I am lost to myself in Christ.

The character of this relationship with God through the Spirit of God is described more fully later in chapter 8: "For all who are led by the Spirit of God are children of God. For you did not receive a spirit of slavery to fall back into fear, but you have received a spirit of adoption. When we cry, 'Abba! Father!' [Abba ho pater] it is that very Spirit bearing witness with our spirit that we are children of God, and if children, then heirs, heirs of God and joint heirs with Christ—if, in fact we suffer with him so that we may also be glorified with him [eiper sumpaschomen hina kai sundoxasthomen]" (Romans 8:14–17). Here again the mirifica commutatio: the God of glory united with humanity in suffering so that through his suffering humanity might be united with him in glory. Here one sees the intractable linkage between suffering (unto death) and belonging to God in Christ. But above all, here Paul portrays the character of the divine-human relationship as an adoption to the status of children of God, "heirs of God and joint heirs with Christ," through the power of the Holy Spirit, who is identified as "the spirit of adoption," the one who accomplishes this relationship. And so we are discovered to ourselves only and always subsequent to our death in and into Christ, in a way that opens to us an entirely new way of speaking of ourselves in relationship to God, the other who is every bit the other, wholly an-Other.

In his attempt to speak of the character of relationship with an-other (the "*Eros*, strong as death") Emmanuel Levinas counters the Platonic understanding of relationship—as relationship with the Ideal—with a quality of relatedness that while transcendent is not Idealist; that is, while it can only be understood under the rubric of what Levinas calls "Mystery" (as the name of the identity of the other), it is not a relationship whose primary object is outside or beyond historical existence.[41] "[T]he relationship with the other is a relationship with a Mystery. The other's entire being is constituted by its exteriority, or rather its alterity, for exteriority is a property of space and leads the subject back to itself through light."[42] The mystery of the other as Mystery is heightened when Levinas turns to a consideration of the kind of relationship that exists through the fecundity of the parent.

> Paternity [and could we not also, and perhaps even more powerfully, say Maternity] is the relationship with a stranger who, entirely while being Other, is myself, the relationship of the ego with a myself who is none the less a stranger to me. The son, in effect, is not simply my work, like a poem or an artifact, neither is he my property. Neither the categories of power nor those of having can indicate the relationship with the child. Neither the notion of cause nor the notion of ownership permit one to grasp the fact of fecundity. I do not *have* my child; I *am* in some way my child. But the words "I am" here have a significance different from an Eleatic or Platonic significance. There is a multiplicity and a transcendence in this very "to exist," a transcendence that is lacking in even the boldest existentialist analyses. Then again, the son is not any event whatsoever that happens to me—example, my sadness, my ordeal,

or my suffering. The son is an ego, a person. Lastly, the alterity of the son is not that of an alter ego. Paternity is not a sympathy through which I can put myself in the son's place. It is through my being, not through sympathy, that I am my son. . . . Paternity is not simply the renewal of the father in the son and the father's merger with him, it is also the father's exteriority in relation to the son, a pluralist existing.[43]

The freedom from slavery (slavery under the burden of the law of death), that Paul speaks of is the freedom to live as "children of God," as a result of God's divine fecundity through the Spirit. According to Paul this freedom entails a participation in the "sonship" [*huiothesias*] of Jesus Christ whose own union with God the Father does not diminish the particularity of the divine child or the divine parent. Correspondingly, we participate through the Spirit of God in the unique parent-child relationship revealed in Christ; and our sharing, indeed our *union* with Christ, does not reduce the alterity of Jesus Christ in some kind of subjectivist *fusion* between Christ and us (union is predicated by particularity, by distinction, by difference).[44]

When we speak of mutuality or reciprocity of substitution, then, we are speaking of the continuing participation in the life of Jesus Christ who delivers us from the power of death to enforce the immutable law that leads only to condemnation, and who delivers us in the substantial and concrete actuality of our continuing existence, which must be "put to death" in the death of Christ. Paul's reflections at this point do not represent only a christological reversal of conventional anthropology; Paul introduces here also a christological ecology:

I consider that the sufferings of this present time are not worth comparing with the glory about to be revealed to us [an echo of the mirifica commutatio alluded to in the previous verse]. For the creation waits with eager longing for the revealing of the children of God; for the creation was subjected to futility, not of its own will but by the will of the one who subjected it, in hope that the creation itself will be set free from its bondage to decay and will obtain the freedom of the glory of the children of God. We know that the whole creation has been groaning in labor pains until now, and not only the creation but we ourselves, who have the first fruits of the Spirit, groan inwardly while we wait for adoption, the redemption of our bodies (Romans 8:18–23).

Paul will not allow a dichotomy between the deliverance of individual persons and the deliverance of nature; all of creation awaits "the revealing of the children of God" because creation's deliverance depends upon this "revealing." And (in Romans 8:18), "the glory to be revealed" ("*doxan apokaluphthēnai*"), to which our present sufferings are not worthy of comparison, will be revealed, we should note, "eis hemas." The phrase can be played loosely, conveying both a revelation "to us" and, more provocatively, "in us." We "expect" ("*apokaradokia*," "eagerly" or even "anxiously expect") the apocalypse of the children of God. And the expectant longing that Paul describes as "groaning in labor pains" is suffered not only by creation but by humanity. The redemption, furthermore, that is for humanity and creation is not "spiritual" in any Platonic sense; it is *embodied* redemption, *historical* and *particular*, an occurrence in the realm of nature; its transcendence is not idealistically displaced. Whatever it means to be "children of God," it does not mean a privatization of the spirit or a flight from the Pontus of human responsibility.

Earlier, Romans had countered specifically the charge of antinomianism: "What then are we to say? Should we continue in sin in order that grace may abound? By no means! [mē genoito]. How can we who died to sin go on living in it?" (Romans 6:1–2) It is at this point that Paul speaks of our being baptized into Christ Jesus, which sacramentally communicates our baptism into his death (Romans 6:3). Krister Stendahl notes that Paul's reference to baptism in this context is "out of the blue" and "quite rare." Paul introduces baptism here "by playing on the Greek connotation of the word *baptizestai*, which means to drown. Baptism is a word for dying, a word for shipwreck. In Hellenistic Greek it meant death."[45]

We are soaked to the skin in the death of Christ. Our union with Christ drips from us. We never "get over" this immersion; this drowning in Christ's death marks us daily; it marks us out, "names" us to the world and to one another as "children of God"; we are shipwrecked, run aground on the death of Christ; we trail wet footprints of this drenching wherever we go; we never dry off. Baptism is the continental divide, the absolute division in the topography of Christian existence: "we have been buried with him by baptism into death, so that, just as Christ was raised from the dead by the glory of the Father, so we too might walk in newness of life" (Romans 6:4). And in this way, baptism is set as a seal upon our hearts for a love strong as death, and as the sign of our paradoxical existence in Christ, our lostness to ourselves, which is also our salvation because it consists in our being called to die in Christ.

When Paul speaks of the baptismal death that defines for us responsibility (and Paul's discussion of the relationship between law, sin, and death is certainly a discussion of the relationship between baptism, death, and responsibility), he does not speak simply of the cessation of biological life and consciousness that all human beings share as an inevitability. Rather, he writes, "we have been united with him in a death *like* his" (the actual phrase is even stronger: "to homoiomati tou thanatou autou," "in the likeness, or similitude, of his death") (Romans 6:5a). Our consciousness of the death of Christ as telos and terminus of our own existence, of which our baptism is the communication, reframes the question of our responsibility.

When Heidegger (through Derrida) says that "the mortal oneself of the *Jemeinigkeit* is originary and 'nonderivable,' it is indeed the place in which the call [*Ruf*] is heard and in which responsibility comes into play," we are compelled to say that "the mortal oneself" of the oneself *who is Jesus Christ* is for the Christian the originary and non-derivable in whom we find ourselves as "the mortal oneself of the *Jemeinigkeit*," and that it is in so doing that we are given freedom from the monotonous repetition of failure, that "law of sin and death" that is the moral destiny of those who seek to resolve their responsibility in their own capability, in the face of their own death.[46]

As Derrida moves beyond his comments on Heidegger and returns to his reflections on Jan Patŏcka's *Heretical Essays on the History of Philosophy,* to which I have already alluded, one finds his most important contribution to our understanding of responsibility in light of our union with Christ.

> On what condition is responsibility possible? On the condition that the Good no longer be a trascendental objective, a relation between objective things, but the relation to the other, a response to the other; an experience of personal goodness and a movement of intention. . . . On what condition does goodness exist beyond all calculation? On the condition that goodness forget itself, that the movement be a movement of the gift that renounces itself, hence a movement of infinite love. Only infinite love can renounce itself and, in order to *become finite,* become incarnated in order to love the other, to love the other as a finite other. This gift of infinite love comes from someone and is addressed to someone; responsibility demands irreplaceable singularity. Yet only death or rather the apprehension of death can give this irreplaceability, and it is only on the basis of it that one can speak of a responsible subject, of the soul as conscience of self, of myself, etc. We have thus deduced the possibility of a mortal's accession to responsibility through the experience of his irreplaceability, that which an approaching death or the approach of death gives him. But the mortal thus deduced is someone whose very responsibility requires that he concern himself not only with an objective Good but with a gift of infinite love, a goodness that is forgetful of itself. There is thus a structural disproportion or dissymmetry between the finite and responsible mortal on the one hand and the goodness of the infinite gift on the other hand. One can conceive of this disproportion without assigning to it a revealed cause or without tracing it back to the event of original sin, but it inevitably transforms the experience of responsibility into one of guilt: I have never been and never will be up to the level of this infinite goodness nor up to the immensity of the gift, the frameless immensity that must in general define (in-define) a gift as such. This guilt is originary, like original sin. Before any fault is determined, I am guilty inasmuch as I am responsible.[47]

In the face of our death, and the gift of our particularity, uniqueness, and irreplaceability that death gives us, we know ourselves as guilty. But, tragically, this is all. Death conceived outside the death of Christ reveals to us only our lack of responsibility, our unresponsiveness to the moral value of the "ought," and our failure at self-forgetfulness in the face of an-Other, with which our death also confronts us. But, in light of what I have said in reflection on the Pauline texts concerning our union with

Christ in his death and life, is it not possible and necessary to say that the infinite love (of which Derrida speaks) that renounces itself, becomes finite and incarnate in order to love the other, performs its primary act of self-abasement in uniting with us and allowing those who are guilty to participate in it, to enact the responsibility that is not our own but that belongs to the other who remains tenaciously and wholly other? This is the good news of St. Paul's gospel.

But is this responsible? Would not such an incarnate love act promiscuously and irresponsibly by giving its responsibility to those who are not responsible? Would not, therefore, the very act of self-lessness and self-forgetfulness of this incarnate love (that which defines it as love)—its giving away the gift of its own response (which was its life as incarnate love) to those who do not or will not respond—be an act of supreme irresponsibility?

The paradox describes the prodigal character of the God that Jesus Christ reveals. But, as the Pauline texts indicate, our union with Jesus Christ does not consist in a fiddling of accounts (what earlier divines called a legal fiction); this union is the act of the Holy Spirit. We are called to responsibility in Christ. We are called to actively participate in Christ's responsibility, which means that our union with Christ necessitates a kind of dying as a way of living and a kind of rising that is an actual sharing in Christ's self-lessness and self-forgetfulness, the denial that is a betrayal of survival even as it is also a living into a hope of the power of resurrection that is not in its own grasp. Our singularity remains intact in Christ. Christ comes to each of us and calls each of us; and his call is always, as Bonhoeffer says, "to come and die." And the possibility of this death is a death in the future of each of us. But whereas the law of sin and death, and the condemnation implicit in this law, was a dead end, the call of Christ to come and die is alive with possibility, it is a death toward life, but it is never a life toward survival. This possibility is the scandal of the church, a scandal in the face of our creaturely mortality, which mortality is merely inevitable.

This brings us back, does it not, to the Marcan passage, and to an awareness that the presence of Peter, in every gospel narrative in which he appears, conveys ecclesiological significance? The ecclesiological significance of the passage is further heightened by Jesus' unusual inclusion of the crowd: "Kai proskalesamenos ton ochlon sun tois mathetais," literally, "and having called together the crowd together with the disciples." Pheme Perkins writes, "This act represents a striking reversal of the usual pattern in which Jesus withdraws from the crowd to instruct his disciples."[48] The saying that follows carries the burden of an invitation and a warning to all those who hear. If this is a secret, it is not whispered. Its hiddenness is not hindered by exposure. "He called the crowd with his disciples, and said to them, 'If any want to become my followers, let them deny themselves, and take up their cross and follow me. For those who want to save their life will lose it, and those who lose their life for my sake, and for the sake of the gospel, will save it'" (Mark 8:34–35).

This passage is followed immediately by one of the most well-known pronouncements in Scripture: "For what will it profit to gain the whole world and forfeit their life?" The Authorized Version actually comes closer than the NRSV in capturing the sense of this passage: "For what shall it profit a man, if he shall gain the whole world and lose his own soul?" Singularity is preserved here in the Elizabethan English as it was conveyed in the Koine. What is contrasted here is one's survival and one's life; clinging, grasping, relentlessly taking hold of existence versus a living that ironically and paradoxically consists in a self-forgetfulness, certainly in a survival-forgetfulness, that appears irresponsible.

The text asks (as a rhetorical question!): What does it profit to survive and, more than to survive, to accumulate worldly power, if in the process you have lost your soul (the text reads, remember, "*tēn psuchēn autou*"), that coherent self or self-coherence and meaning that you believe somehow holds together in your particular existence, the life story of your life? The question bears the rhetorical force of the passage from the Song of Songs, "If one offered [in exchange] for love all the wealth of his house, it would be utterly scorned." A love as "strong as death" is beyond transactional economics; the power of its passion flashes fire, "a raging flame," a blaze that rivers cannot quench, nor floods drown (Song of Songs 8:6–7). What could it "profit" one to gain in comparison to the forfeiture of such love? Survival is poor recompense for the loss of such passion—Passion.

If Derrida is correct in saying (in concert with Levinas) that "goodness forgets itself," then it is also correct to say that the self is good (and is given the life of its "soul," its *psuchis*) inasmuch as it denies itself in self-forgetfulness and in reckless disregard of its own survival. Conversely the self loses its-self in the process of clinging to its own survival and gain ("ton kosmon holon"), in its preoccupation with its-self. The "apprehension of death" puts our lives to the test precisely by calling us to live up to a responsibility that is self-forgetfulness in relationship to (and for the sake of) the other who is the other, the altogether, the wholly other, and "every (bit) other," the other in the mystery of stubborn alterity and not merely an identical replication of ourselves.

Levinas is, if anything, even more emphatic in his affirmation of responsibility, as a kind of self-forgetfulness, in the face of death:

> When death is here, I am no longer here, not just because I am nothingness, but because I am unable to grasp. . . . There is in the suffering at the heart of which we have grasped this nearness of death—and still at the level of the phenomenon—this reversal of the subject's activity into passivity. This is not just in the instant of suffering where, back against being, I still grasp it and am still the subject of suffering, but in the crying and sobbing toward which suffering is inverted. Where suffering attains its purity, where there is no longer anything between us and it, the supreme responsibility of this extreme assumption turns into supreme irresponsibility, into infancy. Sobbing is this, and precisely through this it announces death. To die is to return to this state of irresponsibility, to be the infantile shaking of sobbing.[49]

Is this not the hinge on which turns the responsibility of the Christian in the face of death (as not merely a life-toward-death, but as a life consisting in death-toward-life)? To be infantile is to be unable, as Levinas observes, "to grasp," to take hold and to claim as one's own. This is the state to which death brings us in which the claim "to be master, master of the possible, master of grasping the possible" is reduced to "the infantile shaking of sobbing."[50] To be infantile is to be absolutely dependent on the state of responsibility of the other; it may be termed a form of irresponsibility in that it cannot rest in mastery or even *the ability to be able* to respond. But this "supreme irresponsibility," if we may call it that, with Levinas, is also that which is appropriate to the condition of absolute dependence: the condition of the infant and the condition of the follower of Christ who dies into the death of Christ, is put to death in the crucifixion of Christ, and lives sacramentally in the perpetual memory of this dying into Christ, and therefore is given the only possible responsibility available, the responsibility of Christ. It is ironically our "supreme responsibility" to rely on the other to do for us what we cannot do for ourselves. Is this not precisely the content of responsibility for the Christian?

This is difficult enough to comprehend in the singularity of our own existence, and more difficult still to live up to (as we must inevitably "martyr") when death faces us in and with our lives, and as we face an-other's death represented to us and in us in our baptism into the death of Christ; but it is even more difficult when death confronts us corporately as church because it is here that responsibility is most often defined as doing that which is necessary to insure the survival of the corporate body. To this we must now turn.

THE CHURCH FACES DEATH

Thanatophobia both afflicts and compels the consciousness of the contemporary church, bestowing on death a power denied it by the biblical witness. The church faces death, like all of us. The church has always, throughout its history, almost routinely faced death: as a human institution, as a group of persons historically conditioned and subject to the vagaries of population fluxuations, attrition, and changes of all sorts, subject to the march of ages and cultural factors beyond the control of the church. The church has also—almost routinely—faced more violent deaths, subject to persecution and cruelty, and subject of persecution and cruelty. But wherever the church has faced death, the church has not faced death as those who have no hope, and it has not faced death as though death were only a thief who must wrest life from an unyielding grip. The church has on occasion held life lightly because its life does not lie in its own hands. As William Stringfellow observed in his study *Instead of Death*, "Jesus promised that his disciples would receive and share through his triumph over the power of death. And so it is that his promise is fulfilled at Pentecost." The church is "freed from the captivation of intimidation of death."[51] Neither powers nor principalities, nor things present, nor things to come overwhelm the church because the church knows the power of resurrection, which "far from being the vague or ethereal immortality so commonly imagined, is eventful and accessible for human beings in every situation in which death is pervasive—in every personal or public circumstance in common history." Indeed, the church continues to be liberated from the power of death inasmuch as it is conscious of the political power of resurrection, as the power to raise the *laos* of God in their common life as *polis*.[52]

Under the chapter title "The Five Deaths of the Faith," G. K. Chesterton once remarked on the expertise the church brings to death. "Christianity," he wrote, "has died many times and risen again; for it had a god who knew the way out of the grave."[53] Later in the same essay, Chesterton draws a distinction between mere survival and the power of resurrection. "The Faith [of the church] is not a survival.... It has not survived; it has returned again and again in this western world of rapid change and institutions perpetually perishing."[54] Chesterton points toward the awareness within the church historically that its life does not depend ultimately upon its skill, its wiles, and its wisdom (or as one might put it these days, its executive competence, its technical expertise, its strategies, and its long-term planning); neither does its life depend ultimately upon its faithfulness, theological or moral.[55] The church's life depends upon the power and faithfulness of God to raise the Body of Christ from every death, because its life is a continuing participation in the death and Resurrection of Jesus Christ.

One form of ecclesial life diminishes and disappears from history while another surprises us by being raised to new life. Resurrection is always historically unprecedented, indeed impossible, because it is not a possession of history; it is as unforeseeable as death is inevitable. Powerful forms and orders of the church, seemingly impervious to decay, fall to hubris or intrigue, persecution or time's relentless pace. From the Templars to the Shakers, from Constantinian Christendom to the Orthodox Church of pre-Bolshevik Russia, ecclesial entities ebb like the tide. But to rise again is not so inevitable as the tide—it is an act of the divine—and what rises again does not always resemble what was placed in the sepulchers of the past. Entire movements of the church are hunted down and expurgated from history, while other movements within and of the church simply drift over the brink of the historical cataract and disappear into the currents below. When the church renders its life to God in death, it does not hold onto survival and it cannot count on resurrection as an indemnity.

The church faces death. And in facing death the church's attention focuses, its senses sharpen, its perspective improves. Or, I should say, these possibilities may coincide with the church's confrontation with death. Death can give these good gifts to the church, but this largely depends on the kind of death and the response of the church. Death can catalyze us to hear and respond to the words of the evangelist, the words I have already quoted from Saint Mark:

Then he began to teach them that the Son of Man must undergo great suffering, and be rejected by the elders, the chief priests, and the scribes, and be killed, and after three days rise again. He said all this quite openly. And Peter took him aside and began to rebuke him. But turning and looking at his disciples, he rebuked Peter and said, "Get behind me, Satan! For you are setting your mind not on divine things but on human things." He called the crowd with his disciples, and said to them, "If any want to become my followers, let them deny themselves and take up their cross and follow me. For those who want to save their life will lose it, and those who lose their life for my sake, and for the sake of the gospel, will save it. For what will it profit them to gain the whole world and forfeit their life? Indeed, what can they give in return for their life? Those who are ashamed of me and of my words in this adulterous and sinful generation, of them the Son of Man will also be ashamed when he comes in the glory of his Father with the holy angels." (Mark 8:31–38)

Is this not the historically redundant choice of the church, which is nonetheless always a theological-political innovation that is both counterintuitive and countercultural when faced, the choice between scribing and de-scribing church, the choice between bondage and freedom, between idolatry (of this "adulterous generation" in the Marcan text) and iconoclasm, between losing our souls in seeking the world and gaining our lives by losing ourselves and so relativizing the world's claim on us, between captivity to the powers and threats of death and eternal life through the portals of death? To face death may mean that we dread God, grasp trembling at survival, and cling remorsefully to whatever bloodless thing promises another day like yesterday. But facing death does hold the possibility—in earnest recognition of the impossible possibility of God—that the church may, in fact, face up to its identity, its vocation, and its responsibility, may own its baptism and offer up its existence in the Spirit of Christ.

What Derrida says of the individual death is even more true of the death of the church as Body of Christ: "[T]he apprehension of death can give this irreplaceability" on the basis of which alone we can "speak of a responsible self."[56] For what other reason do we exist as the Corpus Christi, this communio lectionis, this community of the words of the Word, but to pour out our common life in response to the call of Christ our Head? In so doing we participate in the suffering and death of Christ. This mission is who we are.

The irony, of course, is that each Eucharistic feast the church celebrates prepares it and calls it to do precisely this, to offer itself up in the Spirit of Christ and thereby to embrace its unique and irreplaceable identity in the world of which it is reminded in the sacraments. The church meets its death in the death of Christ at the Lord's Table. It consumes and is nourished by the continual self-offering of Christ. It feeds on Christ's body and blood. Yet the church does not seem to anticipate its own consumption, its own offering, its sacrifice when it moves from liturgy to political externality, from poetry to prose. But the Marcan text does anticipate it: "If any want to become my followers, let them deny themselves and take up their cross and follow me."

"*Their* cross." So translates the NRSV in its attempt to speak more inclusively, to avoid the third person singular possessive (masculine) "his" or the apparently unthinkable scandal of the third person singular (feminine) "her" or the vacuity of the impersonal "its." In translating the passage in the third person plural, the NRSV has stumbled into the truth of the corporate hearing of this text that has had its own life every time the worshiping community has gathered round it:

The church has crosses to take up and on which to suffer for the sake of Christ.

The church is an offering, a sacrifice, as Corpus Christi.

The church has its own deaths to die Eucharistically.

The church is, as we individually are, baptismally drenched in the death of Christ. We participate in his death in the midst of our life and prepare for our death through the power of his resurrection. The church's vocation issues from the baptismal fount. Christ calls us from the common table. And so the Marcan text has Jesus speaking with James and John, the sons of Zebedee, as follows: "'Are you able to drink the cup that I drink, or be baptized with the baptism that I am baptized with?' And they replied, 'We are able.' Then Jesus said to them, 'The cup that I drink you will drink; and with the baptism with which I am baptized, you will be baptized'" (Mark 10:38b–39). The church has heard these questions addressed to it—and addressed to it *as church*—wherever it has gathered to worship in common.

Then how is it that one sounds heretical in saying that the church also faces death? Is baptism not the seal set upon the sign that is the church? Is death—is this particular formal quality of death represented in the cross—not the emblem of the church? Does the church not die here? *Should* the church not die here? And should the church not also leave its future in the hands of God alone? And in doing this and this above all else and beside all else—follow? Is the call of Christ, as Bonhoeffer said, "to follow Christ and die," also and even primarily addressed to the church?

Eduard Schweizer has said that "discipleship excludes all other ties." And so the sayings of Jesus about his homelessness frighten the church, perhaps, more than any other sayings in the gospel narratives. The homeless church is not only a dislocated church, but—perhaps even more frightening—it is a church without allies and therefore a church that cannot shake loose its alien reputation. This explains in part why Jesus' remarks in response to the scribe (who said, "Teacher, I will follow you wherever you go"), "the Son of Man has nowhere to lay his head" (Matthew 8:19–22) is connected so closely with his startling words in response to "another of his disciples": "Follow me, and leave the dead to bury their own dead" (Luke 9:57–60).[57] The church seems called to a precarious and pernicious mode of vagrancy, an existence that exhibits "no visible means of support."[58] The faithful church is of necessity the *ecclesia derelicta*.

But is it not possible that the church is apprehensive to follow and die because it has not made its choice between the consequences held in tension in the words of Christ? "For those who want to save their life will lose it, and those who lose their life for my sake, and for the sake of the gospel, will save it." Is it not also possible that this is why the church struggles against and denies death, institutional death, commercial death, financial death, hierarchical death, political death, programmatic death, the death of that which is seen and touched and felt? And is this not why even to speak of the death of the church is often greeted with anger and claims that one who raises such ideas is irresponsible, because the church *is* faced with death, and death questions vocation, and vocation calls the church to a responsibility that is an absolute dependence on the faithful God, a quality of trust that appears irresponsible to those preoccupied with institutional survival? But was the church not made for this purpose—this vocation?

This vocation stands in judgment of us at death as it stands in judgment of us at baptism. For the church to live toward death is for the church to render to God its life with nothing in its hands, nothing to recommend it, nothing to guarantee its future, because at death all guarantees of future are exempted, all bets are off. This is, in part, the argument Reinhold Niebuhr makes toward the close of *Moral Man and Immoral Society*, when he criticizes those who wish the way of Jesus Christ could be reduced to ecclesiastical utilitarianism.

> Jesus did not counsel his disciples to forgive seventy times seven in order that they might convert their enemies and make them more favorably disposed. He counseled it as an effort to approximate complete moral perfection, the perfection of God. He did not ask his followers to go the second mile in the hope that those who had impressed them into service would relent and give them freedom. He did not say that the enemy ought to be loved so that he would cease to be an enemy.[59]

The call of Jesus that issues forth from the baptismal fount at the heart of the worshiping community is the call to follow; and it is for the entire church, as it is for each of the church's members, the call to come and die on a cross. The church that lives in and through this perception, holding with the lightness of a sobbing infant its grasp upon survival, gains its soul, even though it will lay down its life.[60] But the church that is preoccupied with its decline, with strategies and desperate remedies for survival, with the self-serving reallocation of resources and the preservation of party interests, is not immune to the loss of the soul that haunts us as individuals. A death is required of each of us. And of the church death also is required.

As Protestant churches across North America and Western Europe face possible demise, at least the demise of many of the ecclesiastical structures that they have taken for granted in recent generations, what difference do such reflections make? Is it really pertinent to argue that what appears as responsible concern over institutional survival may lead to the loss of the church's soul? Is it even responsible to raise such a question?

The psalmist writes, and the refrain is virtually an ecclesial antiphon: "Offer the sacrifice of righteousness: and put your trust in the Lord. . . . I will lay me down in peace, and take my rest: for it is thou, Lord, only that makes me dwell in safety" (Psalm 4:5,9).

When the church faces death it faces its historical particularity, its singularity, its visibility. This means that every moment of crisis is a moment fraught with ambiguity. There is no absolute certainty, no infallible test to which we can submit our deliberations. Ambivalence permeates our apprehension. But this we know: The call to follow Christ is not a matter of individual piety alone; it is the vocation of the church in its corporate life. While it is true that the reign of God is not restricted to the church, nevertheless, if the church is not the church, its particular mission will go wanting. No one else possesses the church's calling. Ironically the church is most attractive when it pursues its vocation unconcerned with its own survival. But this fact tenaciously resists institutional manipulation.

De-scribing *Church*

Ecclesiology in Semiotic Dialogue

DESCRIPTION AS TRANSCRIPTION

Václav Havel, in a speech he gave in 1989, speaks of the "weird fate" that "can befall certain words."

> At one moment in history, courageous, liberal-minded people can be thrown into prison because a particular word means something to them, and at another moment, the same kind of people can be thrown into prison because that same word has ceased to mean anything to them, because it has changed from the symbol of a better world into the mumbo jumbo of a doltish dictator.[1]

By way of example, he mentions a spontaneous demonstration in which he participated in Prague protesting the selling of a beautiful part of that city to a developer. When one of the speakers tried to bolster support for the protest by appealing to the crowd to defend their city in the name of socialism, the crowd laughed in derision. As Havel explains, they mocked the speaker "not because they had anything against a just social order" but because that word "socialism" had fallen into bad usage and had for many years been employed "as an incantation in every possible and impossible context by a regime" that only knew "how to manipulate and humiliate people."[2]

The relationship between communities and the words they use, their texts and discourses, remains tenuous, virtually in a continuous state of flux. What Havel says of words alone may be said with equal and perhaps greater force of the relationship between words and communities. It is "a mysterious, ambiguous, ambivalent and perfidious phenomenon."[3] Yet the relationship is, for all its mystery, ambiguity, ambivalence and perfidy, the only show in town.

Communities, the word-created social matrices, are themselves word-creators, speakers and hearers, word-interpreters, employers and corrupters of words. In misunderstanding as much as in understanding communities make meaning through discourse and description. And, in turn, communities are shaped and shattered by words. Behind the puzzling inky marks on animal hide and rag and wood pulp, and echoing through the sonic interplay that whispers or thunders on our eardrums, communities exist. Words move among us from meaning to meaning like murmurs rippling through a crowd. Words describe, but, rather than being *put down* with literal exactness, description becomes transcription; words are liberated from their utterance and like noisy adolescents move out of their parents' house to begin life on their own. Every word is encoded with a declaration of independence from its speaker, or, perhaps better, with articles of secession. From moment to moment, context to context, mouth to ear to pen to page, words move, accepting, then resisting, the social stations they are assigned. Some kind of prison awaits those who do not discern and anticipate the movement of words, the movement of those who use the words and using them transform them in the process of describing. And so Havel writes:

> No word—at least not in the rather metaphorical sense I am employing the word "word" here—comprises only the meaning assigned to it by an etymological dictionary. Every word also reflects the person who utters it, the situation in which it is uttered, and the reason for its utterance. The same word can, at one moment, radiate great hope; at another, it can emit lethal rays. The same word can be true at one moment and false the next, at one moment illuminating, at another, deceptive. On one occasion it can open up glorious horizons, on another, it can lay down the tracks to an entire archipelago of concentration camps. The same word can at one time be the cornerstone of peace, while at another, machine-gun fire resounds in its every syllable.[4]

Even, maybe especially, the words of Jesus Christ are not immune to transcription. From the beginning of his address, Havel allows the concept of "Word of God" to play upon his mind, connecting the creative Word as source of all that exists with the creativity of human speech, that "miracle," as he describes it, which "is the key to the history of mankind."[5] Yet this miracle that lies at the "beginning of everything," to which "we owe the fact that we are human," is also "a pitfall and a test, a snare and a trial."[6]

Now Havel asks whether we should regard Jesus Christ's words as "the beginning of an era of salvation" and "among the most powerful cultural impulses in the history of the world" or whether we should consider his words as the "spiritual source" of such holocausts as "the crusades, inquisitions," and "the cultural extermination of the American Indians."[7] The words of Jesus were uttered, and once uttered were liberated to an alarming degree from the intentions of the speaker. Whatever they originally may or may not have meant, they now may be "taken" many ways, depending upon this variable or that, this context or the other, this person's experience or the experience of another.

The words of Jesus, once spoken, though they were drawn from the communities of discourse in which Jesus participated, took on their own life, to some degree, were heard and transcribed by the early Christian communities of faith, and eventually were recontextualized in canonical settings and put to use in ways that may have been alien to the speaker. The linguistic phenomenon of word-creation, though it is certainly not creation ex nihilo, nonetheless occurs in a manner analogous to the creation of the world, which, once created, took up its place as creature over against creator, even though it continues at every moment to be sustained in absolute dependence upon God for its being, like a piece of down floating on the breath of God.

How can God's grace be so promiscuously excessive as to allow that which is not-God to continue in the radicality of free existence? The world is God's ornament of Word-creation, but even while it is spoken into existence, moment to moment, by the eternally uttered Word, it can defy God, else there is no love. Our words are our words, but at every turn they may defy us.

The Johannine author writes:

> In the beginning was the Word. And the Word was with God. And the Word was God. He was in the beginning with God. All things came into being through him, and without him not one thing came into being. What has come into being in him was life, and the life was the light of all people. The light shines in the darkness and the darkness did not overcome it. . . . He was in the world, and the world came into being through him; yet the world did not know him. He came to what was his own, and his own people did not accept him. (John 1:1–5, 10–11)

The relationship between word and creation, according to this witness, is inextricable. But so is the relationship between word and chaos.

Word and order, yes. But also word and anarchy. The relative autonomy of God's creation both threatens and promises creation.

The Word who was God is in relationship to the God who speaks Word, but the two are not merely synonymous (are they?), not if we are to believe the testimony of the Johannine community.[8] To speak and to be spoken is the problem of words; and the dilemma of speakers is to speak and to risk being abandoned by the words spoken. The incarnation reflects this essential risk of creation, and God redeems fallen creation precisely in bearing this risk. But the risk does not cease either with creation or with incarnation; it continues in the risking of Holy Spirit in the substantiation of the radical, historical particularity of the church.

In Dostoyevsky the grand inquisitor who, in vulgar perversion of the gift of ecclesial freedom, moves to crucify Christ in the name of the church, is prefigured in the words of Jesus as clearly as is the church of the martyrs. The destructive risk of the Word lies hidden within the Word's creative power. Thus in the narrative of the grand inquisitor Dostoyevsky voices an accusation against the Word of God that creates worshiping community:

So long as man remains free he strives for nothing so incessantly and so painfully as to find someone to worship. But man seeks to worship what is established beyond dispute, so that all men would agree at once to worship it. For these pitiful creatures are concerned not only to find what one or the other can worship, but to find something that all would believe in and worship; what is essential is that all may be *together* in it. This craving for *community* of worship is the chief misery of every man individually and of all humanity from the beginning of time. For the sake of common worship they've slain each other with the sword. They have set up gods and challenged one another: "Put away your gods and come and worship ours, or we will kill you and your gods!" And so it will be to the end of the world, even when gods disappear from the earth; they will fall down before idols just the same. Thou didst know, Thou couldst not but have known, this fundamental secret of human nature. But Thou didst reject the one infallible banner which was offered Thee to make all men bow down to Thee alone — the banner of earthly bread. And Thou hast rejected it for the sake of freedom and the bread of Heaven. . . . So that, in truth, Thou didst Thyself lay the foundation for the destruction of Thy kingdom, and no one is more to blame for it.[9]

The accusation is true, this indictment of creation itself: that the Word unleashes violence in creating humanity for community and in placing in humanity the restless yearning that, as Augustine has said, can know no rest until it rests in God.[10] The accusation is true that woven into the pattern of worshiping community is both a kind of idolatry that would destroy the true God in the name of false images and the form of iconoclasm that would do violence to any human whose yearning for God surrendered also to the urge for syncretism and accommodation — which is, in fact, inseparable from our human yearning for and dread of God. Between these two, idolatry and iconoclasm, the church struggles to worship God and to know itself. The terrible possibility of freedom that makes this struggle necessary is reflective of the being-in-communion of God as trinity and is implicit in the essential creative act running throughout creation and welling up in the will of creation to worship *together* the creator.

Whatever it means when we say "church," it has meant at least in part *those who have been called out throughout history by God to worship God.* The word about church opens in the direction of the church's origin in the creative act of God in history, and not simply in the direction of its future. The Second Helvetic Confession describes this "church" that has always and everywhere been from the beginning, quite apart from our institutionalization of principalities and powers and ecclesiastical structures, this "assembly of the faithful called or gathered out of the world," whose existence speaks in its very togetherness of an over-againstness. Its "communion" is also an opposition.[11]

And so, even while Havel contends that he would prefer to understand the words of Christ as words of "salvation," as "among the most powerful cultural impulses in the history of the world," nevertheless he says that he "cannot ignore the mountain of books which demonstrate that, even in its purest and earliest form, there was something unconsciously encoded in Christianity which, when combined with a thousand other circumstances . . . could in some way pave the way spiritually even for the sort of horrors I mentioned."[12]

TRADITION AND BETRAYAL

"In the beginning was the Word." But just *after* the beginning, while the Word is speaking worlds into existence—what is there? There is, then, bloody secession. The church flourishes on a diet of blood, drinks it up, and, according to Tertullian, bathes in it as in a kind of second baptism.[13]

The church attributes these words to Jesus: "Do not think that I have come to bring peace to the earth; I have not come to bring peace, but a sword . . . and whoever does not take up the cross and follow me is not worthy of me. Those who find their life will lose it, and those who lose their life for my sake will find it" (Matthew 10:34–39). Within the message of the church, which certainly takes upon itself the role of self-sacrifice, there is that violence that once unleashed threatens to slay those who might oppose the church any time the church pretends to be a single voice speaking a single word, the church enforcing its own encoding. Herein lies part of the problem of de-scribing church. The spoken declares independence from the speaker.[14] The spoken takes on its own life and threatens death:

> The same word can, at one moment, radiate great hope; at another, it can emit lethal rays. The same word can be true at one moment and false the next, at one moment illuminating, at another, deceptive. On one occasion it can open up glorious horizons, on another, it can lay down the tracks to an entire archipelago of concentration camps. The same word can at one time be the cornerstone of peace, while at another, machine-gun fire resounds in its every syllable.[15]

Havel continues:

> I referred to the French Revolution and the splendid declaration that accompanied it. That declaration was signed by a gentleman who was later among the first to be executed in the name of that superbly humane text. Hundreds and possibly thousands followed him. *Liberté, Egalité, Fraternité* —what wonderful words! And how terrifying their meaning can be. Freedom in the shirt unbuttoned before execution. Equality in the constant speed of the guillotine's fall on different necks. Fraternity in some dubious paradise ruled by a Supreme Being![16]

Words, like the parabolic swine, can turn and rend us. This is woven into creation, incarnation, and church. "He came to what was his own, and his own people did not accept him." The grand inquisitor believes he has no option but to execute a second time this Christ, the grand iconoclast, who threatens the institutional, communal, and liturgical existence of the church. There is distance between God's speaking the church into existence and the church, even when the church is convinced that it speaks in the name of the one to whom it owes its existence. This distance is where our words play at de-scribing.

Ancient iconography portrayed the church, at times, as an ark, the sacred vessel of salvation, enclosing the community of the delivered, the doors closed against the flood. One can hardly prevent leaping from image to image: the ark closed against the destructive, corrosive power of water; the arks that held the manuscripts against the floods of medieval destruction, the words, the texts, the community, closed against that which would erase the words from the pages, that would eradicate community by water even paradoxically while the community was created drenched in the water of baptism. The manuscript arks were the shrines that enshrined transcribed words, words that moved while remaining within their shrines; that which provided continuity from age to age (these relinquaries of texts) with the communities that had gone before provided discontinuity at the same time. And if these shrines, enshrining these wordy, bloodless bones, can be said to provide foundations for cathedrals and parish churches and worshiping communities of all sorts, they are strange foundations, indeed, which move, and may make the walls tumble in upon our heads, because they are iconoclastic foundations that call into question and promise to dismantle all our sacred images, our idols and idol-making, even our making idols of ourselves and our churches, and especially our exclusion of those who will not worship together with us our gods. The baptism of water reminds us of and also washes away the bloody baptism in which we have all been baptized, because to belong to this community means we have blood on our hands. We must take the good news with the bad.

"The Word became flesh and dwelt among us." And the Word by whose creative power all were brought into existence was not recognized, or received, by those on whose lips the Word appeared most often. There is freedom in the Word even from the Word. Any word may disown its speaker. Any speaker may disown its word. To describe the church we begin where the word is put down, on the breath of men and women together, on paper in a stream of ink, put down and let go of. This means, first, that the word "church" cannot be derived from lexicons but must be heard in the separation from those who are church and what they say about church, as they move, knowing that while there is continuity between communities of faith, Christian churches, in the past and in other places, there is also dislocation and disassociation. And meaning moves through community. This means, also, that the yearning of a community of faith for the One to worship, by which God calls humanity out from among humanity, can never be fulfilled by substituting for that One the community itself. The church is not the One. This is perhaps most evident in the persistent existence of contrasting communities that, simply by virtue of the fact of their presence, affirm that any particular community's apprehension is also misapprehension. Contrasting and contradicting communities of faith call one another to account, bearing witness to One who is God through their uncertain and provisional character.

What we are asking, again, is this: "What do we mean when we say the word 'church'?" How can we amid the ambiguities of this world speak of the divine-givenness of communities of faith?

Under the sign of this word "church" we have conquered. True. We *have* proclaimed good news to the poor, release to the captives, recovery of sight to the blind; we *have* set free the oppressed and announced the year of the Lord's favor. But under the sign of this word "church" we have also known our moral defeats. We have enslaved and lynched, stoked ovens of holocaust and anaesthetized our consciences with the wealth of nations.

When we use the word "church," what are we calling to mind? What images come unbeckoned? What hesitant images should be conjured up but fail to come when summoned? Perhaps we can approach these questions by talking about the way the church *imagines* itself through its work of traditioning, handing on its witness to Jesus Christ in whose name we speak our words and under whose headship we function as members of his body, thus providing the church a sense of its own identity and continuity from generation to generation. One way to talk about the church's task of imaging itself through its traditions is suggested by the usage in the early church of the term *paradidomi*.[17] This word appears often in the passion narratives. It is used in Mark 14:10 to speak of Judas's betrayal of Jesus: "and Judas Iscariot—one of the twelve—went to the chief priests in order to betray him to them." The word commonly translated "betray" is *paradoi*, which more literally meant "hand over." Another form of the word (*paredokan*) is used in Mark 15:1, where the "whole council" is said to have "bound Jesus, led him away, and handed him over to Pilate." When Pilate, in Luke 23:25, delivers up Jesus to the will of the mob, again paredoken is used to describe this handing over. And, finally, in the parallel reading in Mark 15:15, Pilate is said to have released (apelusen) Barabbas, but Jesus he handed over (paredoken) to be crucified.

The word is also used in the capture of Peter and his being handed over (paradous) to four squads of soldiers, in Acts 12:4. Other forms of the word are employed in the prophecy of Agabus of Judea that Saint Paul would be bound and handed over (paradosousin) to the Gentiles, in Acts 21:11, and in Paul's report to the leaders of the Jewish community in Rome of his arrest and his being delivered over (paredothen) into the hands of the Romans, in Acts 28:17.[18]

The word is employed in the phrase *paradounai to pneuma* to speak of Jesus' giving up or handing over his own spirit on the cross, in John 19:30. And in I Corinthians 13 one discerns the voluntary spirit of self-sacrifice that the early church recognized as a virtue from the way Saint Paul expresses the admonition to love in connection with his comments on the believer's *handing over* of his or her body (parado to soma) to a martyr's death. By contrast, Paul applies this term when, in I Corinthians 5:5, he says that the members of the Christian community in Corinth are *to hand over* (paradounai) the member of their community who lives with his father's wife.[19]

I have yet to mention the most familiar and ironic use of the term, that being, of course, Paul's use of the word to establish the authority for his preaching. He moves, in I Corinthians 15:1–3a, to the heart of his teaching of the Resurrection of Jesus by writing: "Now I would remind you, brothers and sisters, of the good news that I proclaimed to you, which you in turn received, in which also you stand, through which also you are being saved, if you hold firmly to the message that I proclaimed to you—unless you have come to believe in vain. For I handed on to you as of first importance what I in turn had received." The word "I handed on" (*paredoka*) parallels "I received" (*parelabon*), evoking a line of authority and tradition, one witness standing beside another. The good news is, as it were, gossipped along the line, heard, as Fred Craddock says, in a whisper.[20]

Paul's choice of phrase in I Corinthians 15 echoes his prior use of paredoka in contrast to parelabon in I Corinthians 11:23a, where he instructs the church in the institution of the Eucharist: "For I received [parelabon] from the Lord what I also handed on [paredoka] to you, that the Lord Jesus on the night when he was betrayed [paredideto] took the loaf, and when he had given thanks, he broke it and said . . ." Here we have the richly evocative usage of these terms woven together in the context of the Eucharist: bearing witness to the Christ as a receiving and handing on of the tradition is linked to our calling to mind of another handing over, which was the betrayal of Christ.

To be in the community of faith means that one receives and hands on the good news of Jesus Christ. But in what sense is it true that every handing on is also and at the same time both a bearing witness and a betrayal? There is profound risk here for God, the continuing risk for God as Word in the church: Christ is delivered up again and again to crucifixion; martyrs give themselves up for the sake of Christ; *and* in our bearing witness we also betray the One to whom we bear witness. God makes Godself vulnerable in and to and through the church in the church's act of bearing witness to the God who constitutes the church as a community of others by the power of the Spirit. We sinners hand over the Word again and again to sinners who do what they will with the Word they receive; and in the name of the Word of God we do what we will with the church.

When we speak of the life of the church as the continuing event of hearing and speaking the Word of God, then we also must speak of the church in the radical plurality of voices that arise from the church's particularity. And here Dostoyevsky's frightening words confront us in our lust for conformity in the name of common worship, in a perversion of our common and divergent worship of the common

God into an in-common worship that enforces unanimity or commonality at the point of a sword. We would, it seems, even slay Christ if Christ stood in the way of our enforcement of an image of the church, the church in our own image. The blood of Christ, the blood of martyrs, the blood of those who stand in our way, all mingle together both in the chalice at our lips and in many a slip between cup and lip. Is it possible that it is chiefly in the slip of the lip that we may discover the answer to our question "What does it mean when we say 'church'?" Perhaps it is precisely in the rub between our images of church, between their falsehood and truth, that we will discern what we mean when we say "church."

Worship and Idolatry

Humans simply existing as separate individuals are not the creatures intended by God. To human existence belongs living-space
(the garden), the provision of food (the trees of the garden), work
(the commission to cultivate and preserve), and in particular the
community ("a helper fit for him," Gen. 2:18). This complex description of man's creation implies that people as God's creatures
cannot be detached from their living-space, their provision of food,
their work, or their community. They are only human in these
relations, not beyond them in an abstract existence. A theological
anthropology which wishes to describe man as such, without these
relations, in relation to God alone, is not appropriate to man as
God's creature. Were this to be recognized and accepted, it would
have to cause a complete change in the way we talk about man in
theology.

Claus Westermann

Our humanity is constituted as image of God in community.[21] Our humanity as image of God is physically constituted in a particular space, recognizing physical concerns and limitations, honoring cultural peculiarities of various national, tri-bal, and social groups (e.g., the rich, dark mysteries of Orthodox liturgy, the com-mercial paraphernalia of American evangelicalism), engaging its participants in all sorts of activities deemed appropriate and necessary for Christian faith in a par-ticular "place," and always aware that the humanity we receive is a gift of the com-munity through its languages and its complex systems of associations and symbols.

But what happens when a community that makes of itself a false image consti-tutes us as false image, as merely images of ourselves (in contrast to imago dei), when there is no divine counterpoint to our image-making, and our imaging devolves into idolatry? Here the Decalogue chastens us, reminding us that the Fall is not limited to the sphere of individual morality, that even our communities are fallen, and that however much we value our life together our communities cannot be objects of ultimate valuation and veneration.

Carlyle Marney once wrote: "Our images are ways of worshiping the self. . . . Against this we have a clear directive. . . . 'Thou shalt not make unto thyself any graven image.' But . . . in English this is not a good rendition. It smacks too much of wood carving. Rather read it as it goes: AL TA-ASE LEHA KOL PESEL 'You shall not make of yourself a carved substitute. *You shall not make an Image of Yourself.*' "[22] Marney listens to the Hebrew text in light of Matthew 16:24: "If any . . . would come after me let him deny himself." He tells us again, in another way, that our images of ourselves must be subject to "the insights of the community." We need, as individuals, the correction of "the church's memory of what God is about."[23] But what about the correction the community needs of its own image? How can we as church submit the church to self-image–breaking? In light of *what* ultimate reality are our images of church called into question?

Karl Barth's critique of all political and ecclesiastical structures that attempt to place "a second center . . . alongside the real center" is relevant.[24] The church of the German Christians, for instance, whose God was shaped by a mythological racial chauvinism, was called into question because it attempted to find the identity of the church by using the grammatical formula typical to Christian forms of idolatry: "Christ *and* ———." As Eberhard Busch explains, Barth opposed such thinking "in the very first days of the Third Reich," giving "a lecture on 'The First Commandment as a Theological Axiom.' . . . In it he detected a danger of having 'other gods' than God in every theological attempt to connect 'the concept of revelation with other authorities which for some reason are thought to be important' (like human 'existence', 'order', 'state', 'people' and so on) 'by means of the momentous little word 'and.' "[25]

Barth's critique calls into question any attempt to erect an altar to ourselves in place of the proper worship of God. Thus he also calls into question every attempt to derive authority for the church and an understanding of the identity and mission of the church from any other source than the incarnate God. For Barth the act of *centering* was consonant with the act of worship; while, at the same time, it was by and through the name "Jesus Christ" that Barth deconstructed every human theological utterance that rivals the self-revealing God. To put any creature or any part of creation at "center" was, in Barth's view, to commit the sin of idolatry, worshiping the creature in place of the creator.

But is it possible to speak of idolatry at all in the post-modern context, in a time when many assume that the realm we indwell is at best a de-centered world? And is it, by extension, conceivable to speak of any church as falsely imaged without a centralizing point of reference to God?

In a universe in which God is relegated to the point of absolute mathematical

singularity, to the position of divine "Prior" to the universe or, as Schleiermacher referred to God, the divine "Whence of our receptive and active existence,"[26] we are
placed in the unfortunate theological position of witnessing God's being escorted
off the premises as one might remove a drunken uncle from a party where he had
just caused an embarrassing scene. Or, in a social context in which sensitivity to cultural distinctions leads us to relativize universal claims to truthfulness, we will find
it impossible for any cultural, religious, economic, or political perspective to place
its conception of divinity convincingly at "center" for those outside its own community of discourse and to admonish those others outside that community to submit their cultural expressions to this "center" as canon.

If, however, we can understand God as Creative-Sustainer and Immediate-and-
Transcendent-Reference-for-Being, as we see in Colin Gunton's conception of God
as "the Son and the Spirit, by whom the world is held in continuing relation to God
the Father,"[27] and if we can recognize that to speak of church is to speak of communities of faith that, however different and distinctive, yet are bound together by the
Spirit of the God who has become flesh and dwelt among us, then, *yes,* we can speak
within and among our various communities of faith of relatively true and false images of the God who is "the mystery of the world."[28] And while the metaphor "center" must be called into question because of the privileged claim it makes on behalf
of particular communities against other communities, we as members of particular
Christian communities of faith may and must speak of God in God's transcendent
presence to us, and in God's presence as both divine grace and justice, as that which
calls into question our image-making, because God is the One in whose image we
live and move and have our being.

While recognizing a de-centered status for our truth claims, nevertheless, we may
ask the question whether our speaking of church can articulate an imagination obe-
dient to God and whether we may know the boundaries of an appropriate iconoclasm. It is specifically at this point that we come to certain ways of talking about
imagination and iconoclasm, icons and images, that may assist us in reflecting on
what it means to say the word "church," what it means to attempt to describe communities of faith, and how we can imagine our life together without making of ourselves a false image.

Is it surprising, for instance, that the final straw that broke the ecumenical camel's
back East from West was the medieval controversy over images and iconoclasm? Visual and vocal representation are crucial issues for ecclesiology. But how can a sign
simultaneously be both open and true? Can the church honor the God whose name,
Karl Barth tells us, consists in a refusal to be named while attempting also to know,
to remember, to speak descriptively of and performatively to this God through
sacramental word and act, vision and auditory reception?[29]

In defending the use of images, John of Damascus, during the eighth-century
iconoclastic controversy, argued that the incarnation of the Word justifies and
makes comprehensible the church's image-making. While it is "the height of folly

and impiety" to attempt to "make an imitation of the invisible, incorporeal, uncircumscribed, formless God," it is appropriate, desirable, and indeed necessary to make images of Jesus Christ who was the Word become flesh.[30] John, in his *Apologies*, writes:

> I do not adore the creation rather than the Creator, but I adore the one who became a creature, who was formed as I was, who clothed Himself in creation without weakening or departing from His divinity, that He might raise our nature in glory and make us partakers of His divine nature. Together with my King, my God and Father, I worship Him who clothed Himself in the royal purple of my flesh, not as a garment that passes away, or as if the Lord incarnate constituted a fourth person of the Trinity — God forbid! The flesh assumed by Him is made divine and endures after its assumption. Fleshly nature was not lost when it became part of the Godhead, but just as the Word made flesh remained the Word, so also flesh became the Word, yet remained flesh, being united to the person of the Word. Therefore I boldly draw an image of the invisible God, not as invisible, but as having become visible for our sakes by partaking of flesh and blood. I do not draw an image of the immortal Godhead, but I paint the image of God who became visible in the flesh, for if it is impossible to make a representation of a spirit, how much more impossible is it to depict the God who gives life to the spirit?[31]

Our attempts to make images are grounded in the incarnation. This iconographic work is both a reflection of and a participation in the freedom of God, and because it is grounded in who God is as revealed in Jesus Christ, it is critically referenced to God's self-revelation as its proper source and criterion.[32] Its freedom adheres to the "imageless image of God" who became flesh.[33] This means, at least in part, that while the Word is "perfectly open sign," as Rebecca Chopp writes, nevertheless the "openness" of the Word is never merely arbitrary.[34]

In this regard, Umberto Eco's reflections on the openness of texts is analogically suggestive. Eco writes that for many years he was "haunted by the idea of unlimited semiosis," which he borrowed from Charles Peirce and which constituted the philosophical scaffolding of his *Theory of Semiotics* (1976). Eco explores the possibility that one can describe a text as "an 'open' text," and concludes that a text is "open" inasmuch as it invites the reader/receiver of the words to cooperate in the meaning-production of the text. However, a text cannot be described as "open" unless its openness is "envisaged at the moment of its generation *qua* text." In analyzing Baudelaire's "Les Chats," however, Eco concludes that this particular text "not only calls for the cooperation of its own reader, but also wants this reader to make a series of interpretive choices which even though not infinite are . . . more than one." But Eco refuses to extend the title "'open' text" to "Les Chats" because its openness is of a kind more or less common to all texts; its openness is not unlimited, nor was its openness, which invites readers into meaning-production, designed into it in its creation. Rather, the text admits the cooperation of the active reader simply in the same way all texts do to some extent. Eco's observations, under the title "How to Produce Texts by Reading Them," lead him to say that to call a text open is to observe that it enacts "only the extreme and most provocative exploitation—for poetic purposes—of a principle which rules both the generation and interpretation of texts in general."[35]

We have recognized the slippery nature of words, the manner in which they are received and passed on and the danger of betrayal that lies implicit in all transmission and transcription. Nothing could be more apparent than the fact that there are gaps in meaning, whether unintentional (and, therefore, frequently regretted) or intentional (and, thereby, exploited), between the speaker, the words spoken, and the hearer, or between the writer (whose absence only accentuates the semiotic problem), the written text, and the reader. This is the way words work. But in this regard, following Eco, we do not categorically call every message or text open, though we find it necessary to say that any message or text is subject to some degree of openness.

We also see the relative openness of words and note the openness of the Word of God, especially in relation to creation and church. But (1) is there something about the Word of God that limits or somehow places boundaries on its openness, that leads us to say (as I just said) that while the Word is "perfectly open sign," it is not arbitrarily open? And (2) is there an essential and, as Chopp describes it, "perfect" openness in the Word, which finds its source in the Word's eternal generation and intends to invite us as God's creatures into a cooperative enterprise of meaning-production with the Word?

Clearly the Word of God as "sign" signals who God is. The character of God is fully revealed by this sign because this sign not only points toward God but is God. Thus, while it is perfectly open toward God—the Word is fully God and this fullness is perfect, absolute, and divinely infinite—nevertheless the Word is not merely open to or permissively receptive of any and every meaning we might ascribe to it. One's own "understanding" of the Word may also be "misunderstanding." And so when we say that every time we bear witness we also betray, we are saying that the canon or criteria for judging whether something is true or false lies in that which the sign signifies, in the relationship between particular communities of faith and the God whom John of Damascus described as "the source of all things, without beginning, uncreated, immortal and unassailable, eternal, everlasting, incomprehensible, bodiless, invisible, uncircumscribed, without form . . . God the Father, God the Son made flesh, and God the Holy Spirit."[36]

What I have not reiterated—and that which I must state and underscore—in the present context of reflecting on the interrelationship of persons with texts is the point that Rebecca Chopp makes in a critique of a paper presented by Walter Brueggemann on biblical prophecy, "Texts That Linger, Words That Explode."

Chopp reminds us that Scripture, which is understood in Brueggemann and Paul Ricoeur as "a poetic text," is inseparable "from communities—of witnesses, of interpretation, of praxis, of wisdom." She continues: "Scripture, so to speak, exists as scripture within the greater context of the community. And yet, it is Scripture which gives back to community its own reality as the community receives from the scripture a redescription of reality."[37]

But even within these semiotic boundaries lingers room for the mystery, ambiguity, ambivalence, and perfidy that Havel remarks on and that may be immediately unforeseen and unforeseeable to persons in any particular community of discourse. Chopp understands this. It is possible that a community's way of understanding the Word has been ruled inappropriate and unfaithful by another community. Yet what is judged misunderstanding by one community may bear testimony to the Word in ways that are not strictly excluded by the openness of the sign in the interpretation of other communities. As Chopp writes: "Biblically God is known in the many names . . . no doctrinal or philosophical formulation covers the whole. . . . Scripture is open because of experience and experience is changed and challenged by Scripture. In a sense, there is, in this theology of testimony, a refusal to privilege either experience or Scripture but bringing the both together in the ongoing communal life of faith."[38]

Does this mean that the Word as "perfectly open sign" is subject to a kind of interpretation by democratic process with no higher appeal than the will of the consensus of community? To some extent, this is how tradition in fact functions in the Christian church; tradition is, as G. K. Chesterton once described it, "the democracy of the dead," extending "the franchise" to vote "to the most obscure of all classes, our ancestors."[39] But tradition in the church is never singular. Some ancestors vote more than once, and others cannot elbow their way through the crowd to get to the ballot box. At times two or three ancestral candidates win the same election and hold the same office simultaneously, either against the will of various parties among the electorate or with the grudging or complacent approval of the electoral communities represented.

Tradition, if we may change metaphors, represents a multitude of streams and currents of experience and conviction in a very broad river. Some currents are visible on the surface, others surge deep beneath the visible ripples, and still others bubble threateningly only to harmlessly dissipate their force in whirlpools and in innocent splashes against shorelines and jetties.

The Word speaks into the living experience and among the various traditions of communities of faith in ways that resonate with certain voices and call into question others, that press against and affirm and puzzle and hold the church accountable. Within the traditions of our various Christian communities, dialectics of affirmation in relation to the Word who is God operate; and entire communities of community catholic, engendering magisteria of approbation and prohibition, endure. And this messy reality of interpretation and meaning-production, of imaging and imagining and image-breaking, this "openness" is grounded in the creative act of God the Word.

The Word becomes flesh and places God's eternal being at the mercy of visual and linguistic response and intellectual interpretation. The same processes of community reflection on experience and tradition that stand guard against excesses and misperception can become subject to excess and misperception. But precisely in the vulnerability of the Word of God, in the perfect openness of the sign, one discerns who God is. In and through divine vulnerability we come to know God's character and consequently what it means to say the word "church." God is the one who gives Godself away in the most outrageous extravagance and who calls together a community to worship and to follow God in precisely this same lavish way.

Thus, Erich Zenger, in his penetrating study of the imprecatory Psalms, writes of the manner in which, in the context of ancient Israel, communities of faith gathered an understanding of the character of God through their reflection on the given "images" that represented God *and* their own experience and tradition interpreted in light of these "images" of God.

He explains:

> These are images *for* God, that is, metaphors that put pressure on YHWH by recalling YHWH's own constitutive history with Israel and at the same time, as metaphors, leave to YHWH's discretion the fulfillment of these images. It is precisely the central absurdity of the biblical metaphors for God, misunderstood as something insupportable, that is meant to cause "a semantic shock" that leads to a new knowledge of God. What we are asked to do is to expose ourselves to the incompatibility and insupportability of the biblical metaphors for God, so that we will not miss or destroy the complex reality of God by freezing it in particular concepts. The metaphors for God, with their power of utterance that surpasses the familiar and the obvious, make possible, and even demand, a history of new and surprising discoveries about God, and at the same time offer new realizations and ways of understanding. The fascination and vitality of the history of Israel's faith "results decisively from the fact . . . that they did not retreat from the semantic insupportability of the central God-metaphors into a rapid comprehension of superficial correspondences, and did not surrender the will to understand when the superficial correspondences collapsed."[40]

Our imaging of the incarnate God, therefore, is a faithful response to God, not despite but precisely because of the problematic nature of the endeavor of imaging. It is impossible for simple, direct and non-contradictory statements of description to speak appropriately either of God or church. We need to construct images, structural representations and evocative symbols, that arise out of the experience and traditions of our communities in their enduring engagement with the Word and that point beyond themselves to the prototype—representations that neither pretend to contain the wholeness of the prototype nor feign to vanquish incompatibility, contradictoriness, or insupportability but that analogically invite us to see more than we can see and hear more than we can hear.[41] The openness of God that allows us to participate in this meaning-production is revelatory not only of God's character but also of the character of communities that participate in image-making and image-breaking.

This is, at least in part, why Stanley Hauerwas (despite how provocative many of his ideas are and how interestingly he expresses them) falls short in his description of the church. In a recent essay, under the heading "Why the 'Body of Christ' Is Not an 'Image,'" he argues that the Pauline description of the church as "Body of Christ" should be clearly distinguished from sociological and political "images" such as one encounters in "the ontology of the body so characteristic of liberal societies—i.e., that my 'body' is an instrument for the expression of my 'true self'."[42] Hauerwas perceptively explains that the "crucial" issue at stake in understanding the church as "Body of Christ" is that through the practices and traditions of that "Body" we learn that "our bodies are not 'ours.'" Indeed, "the saints cannot know who they are until we, that is, the communion of saints, tell them who they are."[43]

Clearly, Hauerwas understands the critical significance of the community itself as that which forms and reforms us, and one may applaud his attempt to emphasize the distinctiveness of church as "Christian" community. But to remove contradiction from the description of church, specifically to remove the counterpoint of social, historical, cultural, political, and biblical-theological linguistic perspectives from ecclesiological description, is also to dispel the tension that reveals to us the reality of church as painfully and humanly entangled in the matrix of particular facticity and yet, at the same time, as divinely given.

The community of faith knows itself both as *God's* creature and as God's *creature,* as a historically conditioned fact. This means that syncretic notions of church (and we must frankly recognize them as such), such as the "image" of church derived from liberal democracy, are inextricably woven into the biblical conception of church. One might well speak, in such a purposefully anachronistic frame, of John Locke's influence on Saint Paul, for instance, or Karl Barth's influence on John Calvin. This mixed-bag "church" in which we live and which forms us is for us irreducibly the *textus receptus* with which we have to work. The church we know, with all the scars of its redaction and corruption showing, is the only church to which we have access.[44] And it is simultaneously both visibly and invisibly "The Church."

We see here the ecclesiological counterpart to the continuing reality of incarnation of which John of Damascus spoke: Jesus Christ as heavenly High Priest mediates both God to creation and creation to God, taking into God's eternal being the corruption of our flesh, our frail and fallen humanity, our human life and death. The dissonance of this Christology extends into the continuing work of Christ in the church through the divine Spirit. Thus, any attempt to speak of church must take seriously the problem of describing church through images that are frequently unchaste and unchastened and must understand that this is not an unfortunate theological accident, something we would wish piously to avoid if only we could. Rather, in this inherently risky and unavoidably fleshy business, the character of the triune God, God's divine vulnerability and essential humanity, is revealed. The church—precisely in its syncretic reality—continues as a sign of God's character.

3

Taxonomies

Paradox, Plurality, and the Enduring Genius of Church

THE PERSISTENCE OF TAXONOMIES

The drive to classify phenomena according to formal type is at least as old as Aristotle.[1] Indeed, the need to develop taxonomies (the description of subjects by use of typological categories) goes hand in hand with the human urge to comprehend. The biblical story of Adam implies that "naming" is somehow a common task of humanity. It should come as no surprise that the use of formal analytical taxonomies to describe religion, in general, and the church, in particular, has had a long history, from the simple contrasts of Baal worship versus YHWH worship in the Old Testament to the sophisticated taxonomies of religious social organization in Max Weber and Ernst Troeltsch.[2]

My concern in this chapter comprises a survey of the use of analytical taxonomies in describing the life and ministry of the Christian church. Comparing three representative taxonomies, I shall demonstrate the values and the limitations of their use. The implications of this exploration may be significant for the study of ministry, for liturgics, homiletics, and for practical and historical theology, not only because of the persistent use of taxonomies for *pedagogical* purposes, but also because of the promise of their *practical* use, for investigating the identity and mission of the church in our time, and their *heuristic* use, for exploring and ultimately understanding more clearly the future of the church and the forms its ministry may assume.

In recent years three ecclesiological taxonomies have proven especially persuasive. The first two are academic models, carefully nuanced and rich in historical and theological reflection; the third operates as a more popular model, the influence of which among denominational and congregational leadership has been all the more pervasive because of its simplicity. In each case, the taxonomies attempt to describe the church by distinguishing between various manifestations of those organizations that claim this title. In each case, though to varying degrees, the descriptive task bears prescriptive implications for the current and future ministry of churches. I shall move from the more complex to the more simplistic, considering, in turn, (1) Avery Dulles's *Models of the Church,* his well-known analysis of six models of churchly life;[3] (2) H. Richard Niebuhr's classic study *Christ and Culture*, in which he described "the double wrestle of the church with its Lord and with the cultural society with which it lives in symbiosis";[4] and (3) Loren Mead's *The Once and Future Church*, which calls for a reinvention of "the congregation for a new mission frontier."[5] After providing a brief description and critical appraisal of each approach, I turn to a discussion of the promise of taxonomy, assaying the relative values and limitations of its pedagogical, practical, and heuristic employment.

MODELS OF THE CHURCH

Avery Dulles, at the beginning of his study, points to the value of using analytical taxonomies to understand "what the Church really is." However, the methodology appropriate to developing such taxonomies is not immediately clear, as he indicates: "When we ask what something is we are normally seeking a definition. The classical way to define a thing is to put it into a category of familiar objects and then to list the distinguishing characteristics that differentiate it from other members of the same category." This approach boasts precision, but in such definitions as these "we are dealing with external realities that we can see and touch."[6] When we define it according to such a method, we often reduce the church "to the same plane as other human communities (since it is put in the same general category as they)." This reductionist methodology neglects "the most important thing about the Church: the presence in it of the God who calls the members to himself, sustains them by his grace, and works through them as they carry out the mission of the Church."[7]

Dulles's own method of taxonomy attempts to answer the question regarding "what the Church really is" while recognizing that "at the heart of the Church one finds mystery."[8] He develops a set of models that the church has used to understand its identity as, at once, a "divine self-gift" and a social grouping of human persons.[9] Each model has more or less reference to biblical images and to the favor of ecclesiastical authority in various historical periods.[10] We may describe these models, following Max Black, as "analogue models" or, following Ian Ramsey, as "disclosure models"; each corresponds "with the mystery of the Church" but "is only partial and functional." While illuminating some aspects of the church's life and ministry, each model is limited. "Pursued alone, any single model will lead to distortions. It will misplace the accent, and thus entail consequences that are not valid."[11] However, understood in concert with other models, each model contributes valuable insights to our understanding of the church. Dulles' approach assumes the pluriform reality of the church. While some particular church bodies understand what it means for them to be church in terms of one particular model, virtually every church shares some aspect of every model, and the church universal cannot be understood unless seen through the lenses provided by all the models. Therefore, in order to describe church appropriately, a typology must luxuriate in descriptive models; a proper taxonomy of the church partakes of complementary, even countervailing, analogies, as Dulles writes:

> Each model of the Church has its weaknesses; no one should be canonized as the measure of all the rest. Instead of searching for some absolutely best image, it would be advisable to recognize that the manifold images given to us by Scripture and Tradition are mutually complementary. They should be made to interpenetrate and mutually qualify one another. None, therefore, should be interpreted in an exclusivistic sense, so as to negate what the other approved models have to teach us.[12]

Dulles's taxonomy, therefore, should be construed as an attempt to draw together a variety of biblical and traditional images of and metaphors for the church so as to produce a set of analogical models. Yet, because he draws images from biblical and traditional sources grounded in the life of the church over its history, the models bear an implicit sense of authority and are far from merely arbitrary. Further, the models work together to create a larger sense of the church's identity than any individual image could produce. Indeed, one observes that herein lies one of the chief values of Dulles's models of the church: their conspicuous reciprocity and countervailation. For instance, the model of church as "institution" (the first model with which Dulles deals) recognizes the fact that "the Church is essentially a society —a 'perfect society.'" This model highlights "the structure of government" of the church, the manner in which it orders its life together, drawing particular attention to its "visible structures, especially the rights and powers of its officers."[13] If this were all that one said about the church, our understanding would be deficient and distorted. But Dulles places this model of the church in tension with others, such as the church "as mystical communion." By way of introducing this mystical communion model, Dulles refers to the church as institution, comparing and contrasting *Gesselschaft* (society), which corresponds to the church as institution, to *Gemeinschaft* (community), which corresponds to the church as mystical communion.[14] A taxonomy structured in such a way as to encourage reciprocity and countervailation allows for a poly*vocality* that more closely approximates the poly*morphic* nature of reality.

As his taxonomy unfolds, its subtlety pays enormous dividends. The church is, at once, an "institution" ("structured as a human society"), "a mystical communion" ("a communion of grace"), "a sacrament" ("sanctifying its own members"), "a herald" ("permanently charged with the responsibility of spreading the good news of the gospel"), and "a servant" (dedicated to "healing and consolidating the human community"); and in the final chapter written several years after the publication of the first edition, Dulles adds the construct "The Church: Community of Disciples."[15]

Dulles's evenhanded evaluation of the strengths and weaknesses of each model and his attention to historical data mark this taxonomy as one of the most carefully nuanced, complex, and critically satisfying of such analytical studies of the church. It is particularly in regard to the taxonomy's historical care that one is most appreciative, because Dulles assumes that unless we perceive clearly and accurately what occurs in the historical practice of the church, we cannot properly contextualize and interpret what currently happens and cannot utilize our taxonomical categories heuristically to open up and to explore these practices. Dulles understands that the taxonomy is not an end in itself but acts only as a window onto the reality of church. Without this allegiance to the descriptive historical task, an analytical taxonomy threatens to evaporate into rhetorical flourishes, thus limiting its value to the pedagogical purpose of providing students with a set of more or less arbitrary but sharply focused headings under which they can remember the instructor's comments. The manner in which Dulles employs his taxonomy moves the reader along a trajectory from historical analysis through heuristic exploration of church models into reflection on the future of the church; at every stage the analysis orients one toward the actual church's life in all its particularity.

He writes in his own "evaluation" of the taxonomy: "Under the leading of the Holy Spirit the images and forms of Christian life will continue to change, as they have in previous centuries." A "healthy community of faith," he writes, continually develops new ways to understand its life and ministry, as its life and ministry unfolds open-endedly. "The ecclesiologists of the future will no doubt devise new models for thinking about the Church." He continues: "But what is new in Christianity always grows out of the past and has its roots in Scripture and tradition. On the basis of the relative continuity of the past two thousand years it seems safe to predict that the analogues and paradigms discussed in this book will retain their significance for ecclesiology through many generations yet to come."[16]

CHRIST AND CULTURE

H. Richard Niebuhr discerns the identity of church by focusing on the socioethical relationship between the Christian faith and human culture. He writes, in opening *Christ and Culture*:

> It is the purpose of the following chapters to set forth typical Christian answers to the problem of Christ and culture and so to contribute to the mutual understanding of variant and often conflicting Christian groups. The belief which lies back of this effort, however, is the conviction that Christ as living Lord is answering the question in the totality of history and life in a fashion which transcends the wisdom of all his interpreters yet employs their partial insights and their necessary conflicts.[17]

Niebuhr, like Dulles, recognizes the need to use a variety of contrasting types in describing the church. While his taxonomy remains less complex than that of Dulles's *Models*, it is no less subtle, nuanced, and historically sophisticated, and it is even richer in theological reflection. Niebuhr maintains that the church's relation-ship to Jesus Christ and to the kingdom of God that Jesus preaches creates certain incontrovertible tensions between the church and human culture, tensions that to a greater or lesser degree define the church. His discussion, though quickly paced, de-notes abundant historical detail and reflection, from his engagement with Graeco-Roman culture, the Constantinian settlement, the rise of papacy, the monastic move-ment, Augustinian Platonism, and Thomistic Aristotelianism to the Renaissance, Reformation, Enlightenment, Revivalism, Liberalism, the Social Gospel, National Socialism in Germany, and Marxist-Leninist Communism in Eastern Europe.[18]

The value of the patient historical study behind Niebuhr's taxonomy will be-come apparent as I turn to Mead's historically simplistic analysis. Niebuhr is con-vinced that the church is far too complex an entity to be painted in broad strokes. While the problem of the tensions between the church and culture is enduring, the forms these tensions take are resplendent in variety: the tensions appear, he says, "in many forms as well as in all ages; as the problem of reason and revelation, of re-ligion and science, of natural and divine law, of state and church, or nonresistance and coercion."[19]

The ways in which churches speak to these various forms of tension between faith and cultural contexts articulate the identity of churches, telling us who the church conceives itself to be. Niebuhr describes church, thus, by defining Christ (the one whom Christians trust and follow) and by attempting to trace out options Christian communities adopt in their allegiance to Christ and their relatedness to the various cultures that surround and infuse them. He writes:

> Given these two complex realities—Christ and culture—an infinite dialogue must develop in the Christian conscience and the Christian community.... The dialogue proceeds with denials and affirmations, reconstructions, com-promises, and new denials. Neither individual nor church can come to a stopping-place in the endless search for an answer which will not provoke a new rejoinder.[20]

From Niebuhr's reflections on this "enduring problem" there emerges the aware-ness that the responses of Christian communities to Christ and culture fall into five types. Niebuhr's familiar taxonomy hardly needs rehearsal, except to remind us of the ecclesiological pertinence of what is essentially a sociotheological and ethical analysis:

Christ against Culture

Those churches that adopt a posture of Christ *against* culture may take a variety of forms (some ironically at odds with and embedded in the cultures that surround them), according to Niebuhr. From the beginning he introduces into his taxon-omy a principle of variation and countervailation not only between the types of churchly responses to the problem of Christ and culture but within each type.

Niebuhr understands that it is in the nature of contradiction to reveal, that it is as speech speaks against its own terms of category that subjects are disclosed.[21] He explains, for example, that the antagonism of Christianity to the Jewish culture (out of which originated the Christian faith) shaped the Palestinian church in the first century, while the antipathy of Christianity to Graeco-Roman civilization provided the church in other contexts with something of the characteristics of an underground or countercultural movement (even as Christian faith was Hellenized and Romanized through the encounter). In the medieval era monastic orders created enclaves of Christian worship and discipline—which, incidentally, preserved aspects of classical culture—while in the modern period, missionaries have been known to require converts to abandon the customs and institutions of their indigenous cultures and to accept elements of European culture as Christian.[22] In each case the church defines itself to some extent as over-against surrounding culture, even as the powers of syncretism, accommodation, and collaboration have marked out the boundaries of this opposition; the identity of the church was frequently grounded in terms of contradiction, yet these contradictions to culture were not unqualified.[23]

Christ of Culture

A second type of Christian community recognizes "a fundamental agreement between Christ and culture," and thus its self-understanding as church is characterized by its worship of the Christ *of* culture.[24] Niebuhr notes the impulse among some Christians throughout history to accommodate to culture: "[T]hey seem to stand in direct opposition to radicals, who reject the social institutions for Christ's sake; but they are far removed from those 'cultured among the despisers' of Christian faith who reject Christ for the sake of their civilization." What Niebuhr says here of individual Christians, one can say with equal force about Christian communities. Some churches sense "no great tension between church and world, the social laws and the Gospel, the workings of divine grace and human effort, the ethics of salvation and the ethics of social conservation or progress."[25]

In the Hellenistic world, the impulse toward harmony between Christ and culture was embodied in gnostic churches; in the nineteenth and twentieth centuries the impulse inspired Culture-Protestantism and the various civil religions in which Jesus Christ came to represent the agenda, the ways and means, of the surrounding dominant culture.[26] The eschatological dimensions of the Christian faith, present in many expressions of the Christ *against* culture church, become noticeably absent from churches who follow the Christ *of* culture. Even the "present rule of the transcendent Lord of heaven and earth" is less prominent among such churches.[27]

While the Christ-of-culture church is undoubtedly open to jingoistic nationalism and cultural chauvinism, Niebuhr's carefully nuanced analysis also offers a qualified apologetic for "cultural faith" when he explains that "the acculturation of Christ is both inevitable and profoundly significant in the extension of his reign."[28]

Not only that, but frequently the fiercest critiques of particular expressions of cultural Christianity are made by churches that are themselves culture churches—though they are largely unconscious of the fact. "How often," Niebuhr continues, "the Fundamentalist attack on so-called liberalism—by which cultural Protestantism is meant—is itself an expression of a cultural loyalty, a number of Fundamentalist interests indicate."[29]

Christ and "the Church of the Center"

While Niebuhr's first two types of church stand at opposite poles (though not without a large degree of irony, paradox, and contradiction), the other three types seek "to maintain the great differences between the two principles [of Christ and culture] and in undertaking to hold them together in some unity."[30] While Niebuhr finds it easier to categorize those Christian churches that fall into the Christ-against- and Christ-of-culture types, it is nevertheless true that the largest proportion of churches may be better described in terms of these three centrist types.

Niebuhr explains that some Christians understand Christ's relation to culture in a manner that recognizes culture's indebtedness to Christ while maintaining a sense of Christ's transcendence over culture. "Christ enters into life from above with gifts which human aspiration has not envisioned and which human effort cannot attain unless he relates men to a supernatural society and a new value-center."[31] Niebuhr refers to the types of church that share this general conviction as "the church of the center" (recognizing the in-betweenness of these churches on his taxonomic continuum), and while discussing these central categories, he offers some of his most trenchant observations regarding the need for subtlety in the development of ecclesiological taxonomies.

> Efforts at analysis in any sphere are subject to the temptation to distinguish just two classes of persons, things, or movements. Rightly to divide seems to mean to bisect. Existent things, we think, must be either spiritual or physical; the spiritual either rational or irrational, the physical either matter or motion. Therefore when we try to understand Christianity, we divide its adherents into the "once-born" and the "twice-born," its communities into churches or sects. This intellectual penchant may be connected with the primitive, unconquerable tendency to think in terms of in-group and out-group, of self and other. Whatever its causes, the result of such initial bisection is that we are always left with a large number of examples of mixture. When we begin with the distinction between black and white, most of the shades we are asked to identify will be grays. When we start our analysis of Christian communities with the church-sect division, most of them will seem to be hybrids. It is so with our present procedure. If Christ and culture are the two principles with which Christians are concerned, then most of

them will seem to be compromising creatures who somehow manage to mix in irrational fashion an exclusive devotion to a Christ who rejects culture, with devotion to a culture that includes Christ.[32]

Niebuhr's perceptive critique of simplistic bipolar analyses, while remaining indisputably grounded in a modernist perception of culture, anticipates the concern of some deconstructionist and feminist thinkers who see in such analyses an attempt at bifurcation—and, consequently, vilification—by those in relatively powerful positions at the expense of those who possess less power.[33] His own analysis invites an open-ended exploration of the reality of the existent church; and this is nowhere clearer than in his discussion of the types of church of the center.

We could describe the forms of Christian communities that Niebuhr designates as "the church of the center" as the church that "has refused to take either the position of the anticultural radicals or that of the accommodators of Christ to culture." Put more positively, the church of the center "approaches the cultural problem" from the conviction that "Jesus Christ is the Son of God, the Father Almighty who created heaven and earth." The whole world of culture is inseparable from God and, therefore, we cannot reject it as godless.[34] Yet the church of the center possesses humility in the face of sin's diffusion throughout creation. "The Christians of the center," Niebuhr writes, "all recognize the primacy of grace and the necessity of works of obedience. . . . They cannot separate the works of human culture from the grace of God, for all those works are possible only by grace."[35] Niebuhr designates three types of "the church of the center," which completes his taxonomy: Christ *above* culture, which he describes as the *synthetic* type;[36] Christ and culture *in paradox*, which he sees as a kind of *dualistic* motif;[37] and Christ *the transformer of* culture, which he considers a *conversionist* model.[38]

Niebuhr closes his study with a claim that places his entire taxonomy in perspective: "To make our decisions in faith is to make them in view of the fact that no single man or group or historical time is the church; but that there is a church of faith in which we do our partial, relative work and on which we count."[39] Niebuhr's observation parallels Dulles's statement on the relative value of any particular description of the church in the face of the mystery and divine givenness of the church, reminding us that the church is always larger than our descriptions of it. Yet the church that remains larger than our descriptions stands not as an idealist construct beyond the flux of history but endures also as the church universal in the particular and historical practice to which we belong. The sense that "faith exists only in a community of selves in the presence of a transcendent cause" emerges from Niebuhr's taxonomy.[40] His description of church, here, takes us beyond Dulles; his taxonomy, in pressing upon us the insoluble problem of following Christ in the midst of culture, presses upon us also the insoluble problem of comprehending the communities in which this follow-ship is lived out.

THE ONCE AND FUTURE CHURCH

Before turning to our examination of the relative values and limitations of tax-onomies, I shall consider briefly, by way of contrast, a particularly popular attempt to describe the church, that of Loren Mead in *The Once and Future Church*.[41] Mead conducts his analysis of the church in the context of growing contemporary anxi-ety over the institutional survival of denominations of mainline, old-line Protes-tantism in North America. He considers the burgeoning of these denominations following World War II in contrast to their steady decline in recent years. He con-trasts the past centralization of denominational power symbolized in the officing of so many of these denominations in the so-called God-Box, the Interchurch Cen-ter at 475 Riverside Drive in New York City, to the current decentralization of these denominational offices around the country. He observes the variance between the bustle of ecumenical efforts that peaked in the late 1950s and early 1960s and the malaise in serious ecumenism today.[42] He attempts to strike a note of hope with his recurring mantra, "God is always calling us to be more than what we have been."[43] Nevertheless his book appears to be fueled more by desperation than confident as-surance.

There is much of value in this book concerning strategies for addressing the current ecclesiastical predicament, especially from an institutional and organiza-tional perspective. However, it is Mead's taxonomical analysis that particularly con-cerns us, that which he calls the paradigms of the church, the communal forms of the church's life shaped by the church's mission.[44] Mead constructs a taxonomy to assist readers to understand both what the church is and what the future of the church holds by examining a set of categories that describes the forms the church has assumed.

"Our task now," he writes, "is to look at how our vision of the mission of the church came into sharp focus, shaping the way we organized ourselves and the roles we assigned each other to carry out that mission."[45] Mead senses the promise of a heuristic employment of taxonomy to explore the historical contours of the church's life as a fundamental step toward understanding the profound changes fac-ing North American Protestantism. He begins: "Twice before the most recent change in its idea of mission, the church has been challenged to reorder its under-standing of self and world."[46] Later he writes: "Twice before in our history, a broad enough consensus developed about who the church was and how it related, in mis-sion, to the world, so that a single vision became dominant (although it was never uniformly held)."[47] And he continues, "Twice before the church has faced such a complete upsetting of the old paradigm that life was disrupted and structures were reordered to form a new one."[48]

Looking back over the vast history of twenty centuries of Christian church, Mead finds only two epoch-making, mold-breaking transitions in which the mission of the church was (re)defined and new paradigms of the church emerged.

In the very earliest days it [the church] struggled about whether it was identical to or different from its Jewish roots. Simultaneously, it was trying to be related to and distinguished from the Greco-Roman world in which it spread. Looking back with the perspective of history, we see a paradigm emerge—the paradigm of the apostolic age. Generations later, when the new faith became the official faith of the Roman Empire, a reorientation occurred throughout the institution. Like the first, that reorientation was the church's attempt to relate to its social environment and accomplish its mission. I call the consciousness that developed out of that time the paradigm of the age of Christendom.[49]

As we move through the present period of transition, he explains, the second of these paradigms is breaking apart. "Its successor, a third paradigm, has yet to appear fully."[50] Thus Mead encourages his readers to join him in searching for a new paradigm, a "single vision" that the church will adopt and make dominant. In Mead's account, there emerges a yearning for a transhistorical metanarrative, a single, unified, monolithic ecclesial self-understanding that can universally dominate our conceptualization of church.

In many respects Mead's ecclesiology shares Niebuhr's conception of church as being defined largely through its wrestling with the problem of relating its allegiance to Christ with its living in the world. For example, Mead writes: "For two millenia the church has struggled with its image of itself and its image of the world outside. The church experienced a special pressure emerging from its belief that its Lord had given it a double-edged commandment—it was to engage with the world. . . . And yet it was also to maintain itself as in some sense 'distinct from' the world." The history of the church, its mission, and (one may add) its identity are bound up together with the manner in which it attempts "to carry out the two sides of that commission."[51] But Niebuhr recognized a variety of types of response in various historical contexts to this perennial dilemma and an extraordinary range of possible interpretations and ironic turns of circumstance in any age and place. He perceived a profound sense of countervailing forces, of paradox and contradiction, within each of these types of response and variously among them. In contrast, Mead's taxonomy yields a relatively simplistic chronological conception of the forms the church has assumed in its mission and ministry: the Apostolic paradigm gave way to the Christendom paradigm, which is now giving way to a new and as yet undesignated paradigm.

Dulles and Niebuhr recognize a dazzling array of variety in the forms the church takes, the ways in which we conceptualize church, and the manner in which we define structures, orders of ministry, and institutional life. Indeed, while both Dulles and Niebuhr discern the fundamentally varied paradigms the church assumes, Mead flattens the historically varied practice into a uniformity that, while it fits his taxonomy, does not do justice to the polymorphic reality of the historical experiences of the church.

At this level Mead's study fails, despite the insightfulness of some of his observations of current practice. His taxonomy, by avoiding the rich variety of possibilities for describing the church in ages past, closes off further exploration of the actuality of the church's practice rather than opening up to view that practice so that one may draw new insights and avoid old mistakes. In a sense, the simplicity of his categories of taxonomy and his elusion of contradiction, countervailation, paradox, and irony lead him to miss or to ignore the one thing that seems most obvious about the church throughout its history: there are a multiplicity of forms of ministry that are coming into existence; there are emerging a variety of models or paradigms for church; and this situation is not unique, or unprecedented, but is the way the church is and has always been.

Mead's lack of historical attention, his unwillingness to embrace the multiplicity of frequently mutually exclusive paradigms for church that have historically marked its vitality, encourages the view that the crisis we now face is (as some denominational leaders have described it) "the greatest crisis since the fourth century" and thus increases the anxiety over the situation faced by the contemporary church. A more careful study of the historical practices of the church would have seen, with Dulles and Niebuhr, that the church glories in paradigm-making and paradigm-breaking as it glories in following the God whom C. S. Lewis described as the "great iconoclast."[52]

Within the Apostolic church, for instance, varied and contradictory paradigms composed the church's experience; the particularity of the New Testament's epistles and the writings of the Apostolic Fathers reflect this. Franz Overbeck's thesis that "all Christian theology, from the Patristic Age onward, is unchristian and satanic," because "it draws Christianity into the sphere of civilization and culture, and thereby denies the essentially eschatological character of the Christian religion,"[53] gives the impression that the Apostolic period is monological, antagonistic to culture, and unsullied by human civilization. Such was not the case. Indeed, Christian faith was from its beginning cultural, because faith is as much a human phenomenon as it is divine.

Though Mead's discussion is more carefully stated than Overbeck's sweeping claim, one nevertheless receives the impression from Mead that the mission of the church that emerged in the Apostolic period and the paradigm of church shaped by that mission were much more homogeneous than was the case.[54] While Mead recognizes the rich ferment of ecclesial expressions in the first and second century (it is, in fact, rather difficult to discern precisely how he envisions the transition from the New Testament communities of faith to the Apostolic paradigm),[55] he assumes that "the central reality" of the church that emerged from this ferment "was a local community, a congregation 'called out' (*ekklesia*) of the world." This early church, he writes, "was conscious of itself as a faithful people surrounded by an hostile environment to which each member was called to witness to God's love in Christ. They were called to be evangelists, in the biblical sense of the word—those who bear good news. Their task was to carry into a hostile world the good news of healing, love and salvation."[56] The documentary evidence of the first two centuries of the church simply does not support such a singular, unified, romantic vision of the church. There were some communities of faith that understood "church" primarily in local, congregational terms; but there were also those Eucharistic assemblies oriented around bishops whose significance was translocal and symbolic of the catholic character of the church. In some contexts the church undoubtedly acted as a community of heralds of the gospel. But in others the church utterly flew from the world. Among some the church subsided as a community whose life was ordered entirely around the sacramental mystery, sometimes with relatively little interest in the life of those outside that body. Other churches thoroughly engaged the dominant philosophical and political cultures.

There never was a time when church was not dialogically and dialectically related to culture, not even in the New Testament period itself that set the patterns for churches of the Apostolic and Ante-Nicene eras. The witness of Paul (though he was "a Pharisee, a son of Pharisees")[57] bears the imprint of his Roman citizenship and his understanding of Stoic thought. Even the language about "world" placed on the lips of Jesus in the Johannine corpus conveys an ambivalence that will not allow us to construct a single paradigm purporting to represent the young church in every context. John the Baptist almost certainly stood antithetical to culture, but Saint Paul did not; Jesus stands between the two. We cannot characterize the communities of faith that emerge in the earliest days of the church under a single, unambiguous paradigm. Christian communities were as varied as the human cultures from which they emerged. And more to the point, even a very modest examination of the literary remains from the *ecclesiae apostolicae* demand us to think of "church" under a variety of models and forms: the history of these early Christian communities stubbornly resists the categorization of the church as merely countercultural or even as "an intimate community, whose being demanded that it serve and care for a world hostile to itself."[58]

To collapse sixteen centuries of the church's development into a so-called Christendom paradigm (or, as others have categorized it, a Constantinian or Establishment model of church)[59] ignores the splendid panoply of Christian history. A more careful account of the church's life includes, but is certainly not limited to, the astonishing transformation of the church that occurred in the monastic foundations (which radically reconceptualized church both as an otherworldly enclave and preserver of classical and Christian cultures), the vitality brought to medieval Western Christianity through the influence of the mendicant movements, especially the Franciscans, Dominicans, and Carmelites (which aroused considerable opposition from among bishops, secular clergy, and universities), the dynamic changes represented in the rise of papal hierarchy (which displaced some forms of church and brought others into existence), the conflicts between Protestant schism and Protestant reformation in the sixteenth century, and the resurgence or retrenchment (depending upon one's perspective) of a chastened Roman Catholic Church at Trent. A streamlined account of the history of the church also neglects the attempts to re-order the church in England as Puritan within the context of and in tension with the rise of the state church (in the larger context of the rise of nation states and nation-alism in Europe), the countervailing development of the Free Church movement in nineteenth-century Scotland, and the later subsuming of that model within the Church of Scotland. And, of course, it overlooks the continuing struggle to recon-ceptualize church in North America in which the dominant issues are not—and never have been—merely its quasi-Establishment status but also the driving forces of individualism, experientialism, revivalism, and the forging of a new national identity that have contributed to the redefinition of all major church bodies on this continent, in spite of their pre-American origins.[60] I shall revisit this critical discus-sion in greater detail in attempting to demonstrate the manner in which existing taxonomies can give rise to new and better ways of understanding the church.

Mead's essential intuition, however, is correct: that we can use a taxonomy heu-ristically for the purpose of exploring more carefully the character of the church, formally organizing our thoughts about the church into paradigmatic orderings of communal life, and structuring our thinking about the church so as to project into the future to forecast what forms the church and its ministry may yet take.[61] Mead rightly understands that we must ground any attempt to speak of the church's future in critical reflection on previous and present models of the church's ministry and that some configuration of taxonomy can be valuable in this process of critical reflection. But the benefit of a taxonomy relates directly to how we construct its for-mal categories, that is, how accurately they reflect the complex perceptions of the re-ality they describe while at the same time how clearly—and herein simplicity *is* a virtue, though a penultimate one—they portray this reality through the use of ana-lytical models.

Mead's taxonomy possesses the virtues of simplicity and clarity. Unfortunately, it fails, in presenting clearly and simply the big picture of the church, to describe (as I noted earlier) what some regard as the most striking thing about the church: that the particularity that gives rise to a plurality of expressions, values, and forms in the life and ministry of the church is not an exception to an otherwise uniform state of "churchness." Particularity and plurality represent the glory of the church; despite the fact that there is in every time a contingent within the church whose gut reaction to difference is contempt, nevertheless the church has always demon-strated an affinity for variety, for otherness, for difference. Mead's taxonomy of Ap-ostolic and Christendom paradigms thus fails to illuminate the actual state of the church and consequently fails to open to view the variety of possibilities that lie in our present and our future.

However valuable, therefore, Mead's observations of the contemporary church are—and they are fascinating and frequently very helpful, not least in his perceptive analysis of theological education and the training of church leadership[62]—his study is continually undercut by an inadequate taxonomy that fails to understand and to value the particularity and variety of churchly forms and expressions of ministry, and the countervailing tensions, paradoxes, and ironies that run through the practice of the church throughout its history. A more adequate taxonomy would have better served a thinker as competent as Mead.

All of which leads us to ask: What are the values and limitations of analytical taxonomies in ecclesiology? To what uses can we put them? And what should their characteristics be in order for them to function well?

The Promise of Ecclesiological Taxonomies

Alfred North Whitehead once observed that taxonomy is the death of learning. And a danger implicitly lurks in any set of formal categories. They may become, at one extreme, substitutes (in a nominalist fashion) for an open-endedness toward the reality of the subject we wish to know (thus insuring that we can make no real claim to knowledge at any level). At the other extreme, they will claim an unambiguous, universal, and fundamentally ontological relationship between their categories and reality (thus risking the reduction of reality to a single set of categories—an ideology—that a single dominant system of discourse controls). Univocality in ecclesiological taxonomies is the kiss of death. It gives a false sense of security in apprehending the practice of the church when we have only seized upon a set of categories of our own device. No taxonomy can give us unmediated access to the historical particularity of the church in a strict one-to-one correspondence of reference. But in our naming of things, the possibility exists that by allowing a hearing of the testimony of historical practices we are able to construct formal categories that can be used heuristically to increase our understanding of the church. This structuring of categories transpires as an epistemological act of faith.

Dueling Categories

Only through critical reflection on the historical practice and forms of ministry in churches in their subtle and countervailing complexity can we discern the church and become equipped to speak of its future. Consequently, through the use of taxonomies that pay close attention to the church's historical particularity in its often bewildering compexity and variety, and that take note of the disclosive character of contradiction, we can describe church. The taxonomies we use stretch at every seam; such descriptions, even the best of them, limit us from the start. But we need not regret these limitations.

Indeed, one might say that in the limitations of any particular taxonomy one finds its greatest value; that is, it is in the manner in which a taxonomy is conspicuously self-conscious about its inability wholly to comprehend and describe the church that the taxonomy makes its greatest contribution to theology. Precisely at those points where the categories of a taxonomy do not fit well, where they pinch and raise a blister from friction, one can discern more about the character of the church. This does not excuse poorly developed taxonomies of the church. Rather it argues for taxonomies that one constructs as carefully as possible, taxonomies that describe through countervailing models and types the way the church actually functions. But this also argues that we construct taxonomies with the awareness that the church's historical particularities defy formal categorization even as they invite our best constructive efforts. Even a poorly manufactured taxonomy can be used to disclose if it is used over against other taxonomies to point out contradictions between and within the typologies.

Niebuhr says as much in the closing chapter of *Christ and Culture* when he speaks of the possibility of "interminably and fruitfully . . . multiplying types and subtypes, *motifs* and counter*motifs,* for the purpose of bringing conceptual patterns and historical realities into closer relation." "Yet," he continues, "it must be evident that neither extension nor refinement of study could bring us to the conclusive result that would enable us to say, 'This is the Christian answer.'"[63]

Well-constructed taxonomies help us to understand: (1) that the church makes itself available to our attempts to describe it; (2) that the church we attempt to describe is ultimately beyond our description; and (3) that there has never been a single, satisfactory, all-embracing, transhistorical "Christian answer" to the question of what it means to be a faithful church. The answers that have been "Christian" have been real and partial, pluriform, and grounded in the particularity of communities of faith in their peculiar cultural contexts, and these "Christian" answers inevitably and continually call for more and better "Christian" questions. But how can we do more than simply affirm this insight as a general call for humility? How can this awareness of the value of taxonomical limitations assist us in describing church?

Hawking's Principle of Paradox

In a 1995 interview, Cambridge physicist Stephen Hawking discussed the methodology behind his current research into quantum gravity. He said, "One of the best places to look for new ideas in theoretical work is the apparent paradoxes that occur in the existing theory. At the moment I am looking for just such a paradox."[64]

What we might call Hawking's principle of paradox may prove instructive in our study of ecclesiology, especially in the use of analytical taxonomies. As both Dulles and Niebuhr understood, the complexity of the church requires taxonomies that convey (*within* their categorical structures) paradox and contradiction. When we apply Hawking's principle to these categorical structures we discern that the creative potential to expand our understanding of the church lies not in reading into the history of the church's practice a uniformity (or, even, a harmony) that was never there and trying to develop taxonomies that reflect only this nonexistent uniformity (or harmony). Rather, it lies in detecting the places of paradox and contradiction in our theoretical categories, in describing their nature, and in pressing them further.

As one might predict, a variety of kinds of paradoxes and contradictions arise, including: incongruities and anomalies (both of which frequently point to discrepancies and inequities in the social distribution of power); anachronisms (which often denote an unwillingness to recognize the particularity of the historical moment and perhaps an attempt to justify present values by reading them back into prior circumstances); paradoxes (which in their absurdity refer to the essential complexity of human experience and demand an openness on the part of the observer to embrace contradiction and conflict as a way of apprehending what happens, even when what happens runs counter to previous experience and ways of conceiving and modeling experience); and ironies (which, as Reinhold Niebuhr observed, are "apparently fortuitous incongruities in life which are discovered, upon closer examination, to be not merely fortuitous").[65]

For an instance of working with such paradoxes, let us return to the theory advanced by Mead's taxonomy: that we now face in the crisis of confidence in mainline Protestant denominationalism the demise of Constantinian Christendom. Rather than factoring out the incongruities surrounding this theory, could we not focus precisely on these incongruities? In what specific places does this theory *not* hold together? Is it really possible, for example, to place Constantinian Christendom in the same category of church practice as the Roman Catholic Church of the medieval period (which arguably would serve as the bridge between the patristic period and the era of Reformation/ Counter-Reformation), or the European Protestant state churches (most notably in Germany, England, and Scotland) or the quasi-Established Protestant church in North America? Let us briefly examine each in turn.

In the case of medieval Roman Catholicism (and it is important to recall that we speak here primarily with reference to a "Christendom" in the Latin West), one would be hard pressed to make a case that the practices and forms of ministry of this medieval church were either institutionally monolithic or similar enough to the imperial Constantinian church to be seen merely and univocally as continuous with it. The medieval Roman Catholic Church, for all that we say of its institutional centralism (and most comments on this centralism consist in anachronistically reading back into the medieval period a post-Tridentine polity of entrenchment), persisted as astonishingly diverse in form and governance, and its relationship to civil authority (even in the Italian backyard of Rome)[66] displayed anything but settlement or uniformity. The forms of its ministry, the variety of its orders, the cathedral foundations, the burgeoning parish ministries, all of which had their own centers of power and authority variously at odds and in concert with civil authorities (varying from ruling nobility to those whose leadership grew from their belonging to the developing mercantile middle class), only vaguely resembled the Constantinian establishment, and that only in remnants and vestiges, for example in titles that (like "Holy Roman Emperor") pointed to states of affairs that existed only virtually as legal fictions. From a historical perspective, Constantinian Christendom ended within two centuries of its genesis, except in Byzantium.

Something more like a Constantinian establishment (though clearly not synonymous with it) seems to have emerged during the rise of nation states and the yoking
of nationally based Protestantism to these political states as state churches. There
was clear linkage between civil and churchly authority, most significantly in the
binding together of the principal rite of Christian initiation (baptism) and citizenship in the state. Certain church appointments lay (in Anglicanism, for instance) in
the hands of some civil authorities; the system of financial support for religion
melded (and, frequently, brought into conflict) the interests of church and civil government; and the church, at times, was seen as providing an essential set of services
and beliefs chiefly valued in society because of the manner in which they contributed to the stability of the state.[67]

When, however, we turn to the quasi-Establishment of the church in North
America, we are examining something very different indeed. While Protestant
churches have enjoyed privilege in North America and the civil leaders of society
have been primarily drawn from the ranks of the church, the church has not (since
the colonial period)[68] enjoyed the status of *con*-sovereignty with secular government, nor has the church's leadership been chosen by the civil authorities. While
various teachings of the church have influenced the civil canon of acceptable belief
and behavior, and the civil norms have flavored the teachings of the church (in a variety of ways from patriotic Erastianism to Christian cults that oppose the federal
government), the rites of the church do not function as rites of the secular society
(not even the most common, marriage); and the rites of civil order are held in tension with a variety of Christian beliefs and values (the Sermon on the Mount, for example, stands in tension with the rights and duties of citizens and the "responsible"
acts of estate planning, investment, and insurance).

The paradox or, better, the irony that runs through the Mead taxonomy of the
church is essentially this: to say that the church is moving into a time when Constantinian Christendom will no longer be the operative model is tautological (at the
most rudimentary level of tautology—the superfluous statement of the obvious).
That into which we are moving is certainly not a Constantinian Establishment of
the Church (this is true); but it is not possible to move out of something that, in
fact, we have not been inhabiting. Attempting to examine the ministry of the church
from the vantage point of this taxonomy, we cannot see the most obvious feature of
ecclesiology, as we have previously noted—the diversity and plurality of expression
that have been (and continue to be) the hallmarks of Christian church in particular
cultural contexts. To say that we now face the greatest shift since the fourth century
merely exaggerates the crisis and escalates the anxiety of church leaders while doing
nothing to help us understand what is actually occurring.

The existence of certain institutional expressions of Protestant denominationalism are threatened. This is undoubtedly true. But by focusing on a taxonomy
that gives us only one way to conceptualize the church, we are offered a forced (and
false) choice between either a kind of institutional agnosticism (we are told, in

essence, that one simply cannot imagine what form the church will next take because this kind of crisis is virtually unique) or a radically disestablished, countercultural, and largely congregationalist form of church.[69] While this radically disestablished church has considerable appeal and is a valid ecclesiological expression, it
is not at all apparent that it is the only choice available. By contrast, when we focus
our attention at the point of this irony in the Mead taxonomy we have the potential of exploring further what kinds of responses the church might make, understanding that the church is, if not infinitely adaptable, at least capable of a
vast plurality of expressions—and the church always has been.

We could also employ Hawking's principle of paradox in relation to the taxonomies of Dulles and Niebuhr, though I drew my example from Mead's taxonomy. And it is possible to search for other kinds of contradiction within any taxonomy (for instance, noting the various anachronisms in one's reading of church
history and asking what contemporary values these anachronisms serve to reinforce, by exploring the various ways in which the word "culture" is employed and
the manner in which differing culture theories call into question or reinforce various ecclesiologies).

Open Categories

Taxonomies should never function as ends in themselves, but should act in a manner similar to open signs,[70] linguistic signifiers that make further investigation both
possible and necessary and critically challenge those simplistic models of the church
that ignore the particularity and polymorphic quality of its practice and enforce
uniformity over variety. A linguistically open approach to the use of taxonomies derives from an ecclesiology that affirms the normative quality of God's self-disclosure
in Jesus Christ for its knowledge of God and its comprehension of its own life and
ministry, a divine self-disclosure by which God eschatologically defers God's revelation in the very act of revealing Godself in the incarnation. This recognizes again,
Karl Barth's insight, that even the revealed name of God "consists in the refusal of a
name" that is "still really revelation, communication and illumination." Thus Barth
continues: "God is the One whose being can be investigated only in the form of a
continuous question as to His action."[71]

The church, which in its "divine givenness" is the creation of God, the "body" and
"bride" of Christ, and which exists under the authority and authorship of the Word
and through the continuing power of the divine Spirit, is a living text within the
world and can only be investigated in the form of a continuous interrogation as to
the identity of its action (To whom does church belong?). Any taxonomical analysis
of the church must, therefore, remain open, must in fact sow the seeds of its own
iconoclastic ruin, must resist making of itself an image in place of God's always new
(and always threatening) action in the midst of the church—it has to understand
that God's action constitutes the very life of the church as church. This openness
pays attention to the particularity of the church in the history of its practice; it lis-

tens to the voices of tradition and the continuing experience of communities of faith. Through the contradictions between and within our typologies of church, therefore, we bear witness to the mystery of God's act of creation and redemption of human persons in and through and for community.

The pedagogical use of a taxonomic representation of the church lies in part in the clarity of the taxonomy, in the sharp distinctions between types and models; but the pedagogical value is not restricted to this clarity of distinction. Learning to describe church is also enhanced by the awareness that no single taxonomy can describe the church, that, indeed, the church comes more clearly into focus precisely when we place one set of categories alongside another and discern the play between them.

Through such pedagogy we invite students of the church to enter into the practical and heuristic employment of taxonomies, to ask of the practices of the church in historical particularity how the forms of its ministry and corporate life can be understood, and to explore the meaning of the church, pressing home the question of its identity and mission in contemporary settings and for the future. The openness of this quest for understanding is essential: taxonomies that close the process of investigation are not only of questionable value but are potentially idolatrous. In order to trace the trajectories of the church's life and practice of ministry, we must remain faithful to the God of the church whose name lies hidden in revelation, for whom contradiction makes possible disclosure. Yet we are compelled to name. To construct taxonomies is more than an occupational hazard for theologians; it is an essentially human and, therefore, Christian vocation.

4

Speaking of Church

What Does It Mean When We Use the Word "Church"?

Sign. [a. F. *signe, sine,* ad. L. *signum* mark, token, etc.] I.1.a. A gesture or motion of the hand, head . . . serving to convey an intima-
tion or to communicate some idea. Freq. in phrases *to make a sign
or signs,* and *by signs.* . . . 2.a. A mark or device having some special
meaning or import attached to it, or serving to distinguish the
thing on which it is put. Freq. in *sign of the cross.* . . . 3. A mark of
attestation (or ownership), written or stamped upon a document,
seal, etc. . . . 4. A figure or image; a statue or effigy; an imprint. . . .
5.a. A device borne on a banner, shield, etc; a cognizance or badge.
. . . 6.a. A characteristic device attached to, or placed in front of, an
inn (house) or shop, as a means of distinguishing it from others or
directing attention to it; in later use commonly a board bearing a
name or other inscription, with or without some ornament or picture. . . . II.7.a. A token or indication (visible or otherwise) *of* some
fact, quality, etc. . . . 8.a. A trace or indication *of* something; a
vestige. Chiefly in negative phrases. . . . 9. An omen of some coming
event; *spec.* an omen or portent. . . . 10. An act of miraculous nature,
serving to demonstrate divine power or authority.

The Compact Oxford English Dictionary (1991)

LISTENING TO LANGUAGE

Recently I taught a workshop on the subject: "What is the Church?" I began the ses-
sion by asking that question. Hands shot up immediately.

"A fellowship," one person quickly responded. "A community," said another. "A
believing community!" offered yet someone else. "A spiritual community. Or, maybe,
a community of the Spirit?" "The people of God." "How about a people of God?"

Before long, attempts to speak of the church changed from simple descriptive
phrases and statements to something more evocative; metaphors and images and
analogies expanded.

"The church is a caring community," said someone. "I feel cared for by the church. I want other people to feel cared for too." There were nods of agreement. "It's all-inclusive," a woman added. "Anyone can belong." Another woman said: "The church is a loving and supportive fellowship. I feel like the church is a family, my family. Even when painful and hurtful things happen in church, it's still my family." Someone observed, "I think we've got to talk about the church as a group of people that serves God by serving other persons, but I don't know how to say that simply." "The favorite name for the church is the Body of Christ, isn't it?" a man asked. "That's what I always think of when I think of church—the Body of Christ." "It's called a temple in the Bible, but I've never understood exactly why." "A royal priesthood," said someone. "A priesthood of *all* believers," another added. "I don't understand what that means," said someone else.

It struck me that within just a few moments this group had touched upon virtually all the major images and some of the minor images presented in Paul Minear's classic study *Images of the Church in the New Testament*.[1] It also struck me that within just a few minutes the group found itself in the rather odd position of not knowing what to do with its own speech about the church. They spoke out of a combination of learned and traditioned, at times rote, responses and their own experience. They attempted to make sense of church through this combination of speech and to do this in such a way that there was meaningful discourse, rather than mere babel. The reality of the church—the church that exists in actuality and not merely in our idealized imaginations—quickly proved rather ambiguous and too large to describe with ease. I was reminded of Karl Barth's marvelous comment: "We always seem to be handling an intractable object with inadequate means."[2] This certainly is true of the church, Christ's "new creation by water and the Word," as the hymn says.[3]

To speak, for instance, of the church as the Body of Christ evokes a world of associations that illuminate our understanding of the church; but these attempts to speak plunge us into the valley of the shadow of rhetoric, and one quickly discerns that every revelation necessarily involves hiddenness; that which is unveiled is also consequently veiled.[4] Apocalypse stretches language to the limit because it points us beyond the boundaries of language. Is the church (the body of which Christ is the head) an extension of the incarnation? If so, is it also fully God and fully human? Or is it a hybrid somewhere in between—or is it something else altogether? If the church is not an extension of the incarnation (and I do not see how we can simultaneously avoid idolatry and say it is an extension of the incarnation) then how should we describe God's unique and continuing act of vulnerability plunging into human communities as divine Word and Spirit? If the church is the Body of Christ, in what sense is it?—because we might well expect the Body of Christ to be both divine and human if we take seriously the credal presuppositions of fourth-century orthodoxy that held together just such a conflict in Christology, yet anything we say about this Body must resist confusing the two natures. We are not

God! Can we make any statement about the church directly, simply, and unequiv-
ocally, or does speech about the church necessitate another kind of language, either
a more elegantly nuanced articulation or a more brutally conflicted dialectic, in
which we attribute to the church opposite qualities and hold them in tension in
seeming contradiction?

Avery Dulles, in his *Models of the Church*, speaks of the way the New Testament
combines the metaphor of the church as temple with the image of the Body of
Christ. He writes that while these conceptions are "logically incoherent," their combination makes sense theologically. The church is the fleshy, organic, growing body
of which Christ is head; the church is the product of sacred architecture. The church
is an inclusive whole in which diverse members participate in the common life of
worship. The church is also the holy shrine whose walls remember Zion, the dwelling
place of the Most High. The church, a temple built of living stones, is at the same
time already a completed project; and the body, in process of maturation, is still
under construction.[5] Both images and many others (equally in counterpoint or contradiction) prove true to our experience! The profusion of images of the church, the
variety of metaphors and descriptors of all sorts, as Minear says, "reflects . . . theological vitality."[6]

Henry Chadwick, in speaking of Saint Paul's understanding of the church, writes:
"In particular (Paul taught) the Lord is immanent within his Church, as the soul in
the body, which is therefore ever growing until the final consummation when it is to
be coterminous with the human race itself."[7] And certainly this universal and inclusive (and imperialistic) stream of thought exists in the Pauline literature. But another, almost cultic or sectarian current in Paul, countercultural in its impetus, limited and exclusive in orientation, gives force to the teaching of the church: "extra
ecclesiam nulla salus" ("there is no salvation outside the church"). Contradiction,
the need for our speech to stand over against itself in order to speak truly, is essential
to our language about the church.

Oddly enough, the class of which I asked the question, What is the church? did
not say, "The church is a building in which we worship God." Yet this is commonly
said, and when we think of church, it is not unusual for a picture to emerge in our
minds of an architectural structure—a Norman cathedral, a clapboard American
Gothic, a spired urban or A-frame suburban church. They also did not use church
exactly in the same way we commonly say, "We're going to church tomorrow morn-
ing," in which the word "church" functions as a complex sign for whatever variously
happens when we gather together as a local congregation (worship, Christian education, conversation in the kitchen of the fellowship hall). One might well wonder
what is in operation in our speech that prevents us from answering the question,
What is the church? in a way that honors how we ordinarily use the word "church."
Our theological task, if it hopes to be true to the subject of our theologies, cannot
selectively censor Christian speech but must pay attention to how we actually speak.
The language that concerns us, in other words, is not only the specialized conversa-

tion of professional theologians and those voices of tradition that speak from the pages of scholarly books and that emerge from credal texts; we certainly give these seats of honor at the table of theological discourse, but the conversation is not exclusively theirs. The language that interests us is the total speech of the church, the ordinary conversations of the church in pew and pulpit, the theological slips of the tongue that say more than we may know, taken together with the statements of ecclesiastical leaders and specialists in academic theology.

What does it mean when we say "church"? What do we mean when we use this word? Other ways to go about theologically reflecting on the church, its worship, life, ministry, and mission exist, but my approach will be to pay attention to Christian speech (especially ordinary speech), to listen to our common language. Karl Barth, in his first series of dogmatic lectures (1924–1925), speaks of the promise of doing so:

> This phenomenon of Christian *speaking*, whether by Christianity, in its name, for its extension or establishment, or however we might put it, is as it were the raw stuff of dogma and dogmatics. As such it is our methodological starting point. Phenomenologically, the origin and meaning of dogmatics is the fact that there is talk either by the Christian church or, as we might put it more cautiously for the time being, in the Christian church. The Christian church begins by listening to the address of the prophets and apostles, which was not babbled, or mimed, or put to music, or danced, but spoken and written in statements and groups of statements. Why precisely *this* specific address? Not for its own sake nor for the sake of its bearers, the prophets and apostles, but because in and through it the church thinks it perceives another address, that is, revelation, and through the kerygma, through the revelation perceived in the kerygma, the Word of God.[8]

The church gathers round the speech about and for God, the responsive language that is Christian speech, the language borne in listening to the Word of God that by the power of the Spirit of God brings to articulation God's Word in our humanity. The church is also "a fellowship of spirit and faith," "a fellowship with a distinctive orientation, a fellowship of the sacrament."[9] Barth elaborates:

> [W]hat makes it the church, what distinguishes it from any other fellowship of faith and spirit and distinctive orientation and sacrament, is the vital link between this very specific hearing and making heard, the Word which it receives and passes on. To generate faith God has instituted the preaching office, giving the gospel and the sacrament, so that through them as means he might give the Holy Spirit, who works when and where he wills in those who hear the gospel.[10]

The church is brought into being by a particular kind of speech that has the audacity to claim that it has been called forth (and, indeed, has its entire existence in

being continually summoned) through the Word of God. And, even more auda-
ciously, the church claims to continue to speak this Word of God that calls forth its
speech.[11] This is the act of faith at the core of the church's existence—and it is an act
that is peculiarly linguistic. The actuality of the church, its concrete existence, hangs
on *this* speech and the relationship between *this* speech and God's Word. The faith
of the church, in both the sense of its most sacred beliefs and its trust in God,
grounds itself again and again in the necessity (one might almost say the compul-
sion) to speak in response to the Word of God it believes it hears. Theological reflection on what the church confesses—not least what the church understands about
its own identity and character as church—consists primarily in the church's examination of its speech, what Barth calls the "investigation of the meaning or concealed
reality within the very ambiguous phenomenon of Christian speaking. . . . Dogmatics is very specifically reflection on this speaking with reference to the Word of God,
namely, how far the Word of God is, or is meant to be, identical with it."[12]

But, let us return to our starting point in the answers the members of the class
gave to the question, What is the Church? Are we searching for "the meaning or concealed reality within" their speech, as Barth says? Is it as though we are engaged in a
quest for the hidden essence, the true and eternal and proper imperative of the
church beyond the indicative of the church's existence? One betrays an almost docetic distaste for the historical church whenever one raises a question like What
would it mean for the church to be the Body of Christ?[13] Or are we searching for
their understanding of their words, attempting to discern the way the church exists
as church (as Body of Christ, people of God) precisely in and through its ambiguity, as articulated by what Barth describes as "the very ambiguous phenomenon of
Christian speaking"?

What I ask here is simply this: Are we attempting in a quasi-Platonic fashion to
establish the eternal ideal, the essence of "churchness," against which we shall measure what people experience of church in reality? Or is our task as theologians something else, something at once more modest and more ambitious altogether?

I would argue that the church we know in actuality, the church we experience
in ordinary time, the church that worships in assorted settings under a variety of
names in a diversity of ways on Sunday mornings throughout the world, the church
that argues and mourns and rejoices and heals, the church that endures the pres-
sures to provide services for religious consumers, the church of endless committee
meetings and dirty linen washed in public, this church *is* the church of which we
speak and to which the Word of God is addressed, and through which the Word of
God makes Godself known in and through and as human speech. This is the
church God intends and loves and redeems. And so when we speak of church we
cannot afford to lapse into ecclesiological essentialism. We must pay attention to
this church and the speech of this church. Whatever imperative we lay upon this
church emerges from the encounter between the church that is and the incarnate
Word who meets us in the radical ambiguity of creaturely existence. Criteria for

churchness exist, but they are incarnate criteria — flesh and spirit, water and word, cup and loaf.

Roland Barthes's essay "The *Blue Guide*" is suggestive for those who want to learn to reflect on the speech of the church about itself. His essay considers a popular series of tourist guidebooks (called *Guide Bleu* in French) to various European destinations. To be precise, his essay considers the presuppositions, one might almost say the prejudices, of the guidebook, which remain unstated by the editors and reduce the particularities of a country and its inhabitants to stereotypes, clichés, and sights (or monuments) to be seen, but not observed. The complex and real "human life of a country disappears," he writes, "to the exclusive benefit of its monuments."[14] And the rich diversity of human existence is boiled down to a few picture postcard images. He writes:

> In Spain, for instance, the Basque is an adventurous sailor, the Levantine a lighthearted gardener, the Catalan a clever tradesman and the Cantabrian a sentimental highlander. We find again here this disease of thinking in essences, which is at the bottom of every bourgeois mythology of man (which is why we come across it so often). The ethnic reality of Spain is thus reduced to a vast classical ballet, a nice neat commedia dell'arte, whose improbable typology serves to mask the real spectacle of conditions, classes and professions. For the *Blue Guide,* men exist as social entities only in trains, where they fill a "very mixed" Third Class. Apart from that, they are a mere introduction, they constitute a charming and fanciful decor, meant to surround the essential part of the country: its collection of monuments.[15]

Is there not a corresponding danger in ecclesiology to reduce the vast diversity of church, the ambiguities of this rich human-divine reality, to a few neat (noncontradictory) patterns, types, models, paradigms, definitions, or descriptions—to notice the monumental remains and to dismiss as irrelevant (and irrelevantly messy) the actual communities of faith that shape these monuments and that move within them and make sense of them? What would it entail, what would it require of us, to notice and take seriously the particularities of church, to go beyond phenomenology to phenomengnosis, to understand the ambiguous flux of existence as itself the sign that demands to be understood in its own terms?[16] Barthes says, later in this essay:

> Generally speaking, the *Blue Guide* testifies to the futility of all analytical descriptions, those which reject both explanations and phenomenology: it answers in fact none of the questions which a modern traveller can ask himself while crossing a countryside which is real *and which exists in time.* To

select only monuments suppresses at one stroke the reality of the land and that of its people, it accounts for nothing of the present, that is, nothing historical, and as a consequence, the monuments themselves become undecipherable, therefore senseless. What is seen is thus constantly in the process of vanishing, and the *Guide* becomes, through an operation common to all mystifications, the very opposite of what it advertises, an agent of blindness.[17]

A tourist, perhaps on one of those packaged coach tours, can visit a foreign country only to tick off the sights (the monuments): the Eiffel Tower, Westminster Abbey, Edinburgh Castle. She envisions the people of these foreign countries she visits as stereotypes already firmly established in her head: Scot in kilt with bagpipes, Englishman with umbrella and bowler, Frenchman wearing beret, smoking cigarette, drinking wine. The tourist returns home having traveled but having only minimally encountered the countries toured and their inhabitants. The idiosyncratic, the eccentric reality of humanity, the exactness of place and time and circumstance, the life lived in ordinariness is easily ignored in the headlong rush to account for all stereotypes (thus never really knowing the people) and monuments (thus never understanding why the monuments are there or what they signify). One sees here the way in which the yearning for essence can alienate us from history; though this superficial tourist may be surrounded by "historical" monuments, she has little access to their meaning because they have been decontextualized; consequently, she is estranged from her own history of being present in that place. In the worst cases, the tourist takes her "home" on tour with her to the extent that she never enters into the foreign time and place at all—the ultimate jet lag.

The ecclesiastical tourist, likewise, can emerge from a "study of the doctrine of the Church" having never entered into church at all. While giving the impression of sailing to all the great ports of call, he may have only circumnavigated the stereotypes. What is clearly implied in such ecclesiological globetrotting is that the church is an idea, and that paying attention to the actuality of particular human communities of faith only distracts us from some divine ecclesiology, a neat analytical description that is (supposedly) forever and everywhere true.

The thesis, to which we have returned by a variety of roads (even—indeed, especially—when we considered the possibility of using analytical taxonomies in the description of the church), is this: We must pay attention to the way the church speaks in order to understand what the church is. And in order to pay attention to the speech of the church we must not abstract ourselves from the ordinary conversations of the church's worship, preaching, and common life in particular communities of faith and the manner in which these conversations participate in (and sometimes avoid) conversations that arise from other particular communities of faith. The messiness of these conversations, the fact that they arise from a diversity of communities claiming to be Christian, challenges the most common assumptions about truth, that it is non-contradictory, that it is singular, and, therefore, that it is universal. Conceptions of perfection, completeness, and wholeness are conventionally tied to this conception of truth, so it is not uncommon for adherents to a particular community of faith that has enjoyed confessional hegemony over other communities to protest against the emerging diversity of voices (which means, in fact, that the diversity is being heard, whereas formerly it existed but was not accorded a public voice, a voice that could be heard by others), fearing that diversity, contradiction, and heterogeneity mean the dissolution of church—and perhaps the end of civilization as we know it!

Barthes in another essay observes, in a passage saturated with irony, "It is well known that smoothness is always an attribute of perfection because its opposite reveals a technical and typically human operation of assembling." Christ's "seamless" robe and "the airships of science-fiction" that are molded from "unbroken metal" exemplify this.[18] What if the perfection of the church is its human existence and not something beyond the actuality of this existence? What if its roughness and raggedness, its lack of smoothness and seamlessness, is the shape of its peculiar wholeness? What if, indeed, its limitations, its utter need for God, its spiritual bankruptcy are the infallible signs of its perfection? What if, then, the miracle of truth is that God makes the Word of God vulnerable as human speech, that it is this act itself that is truth (and not something spoken about this act)? And so, what if the contradictory, unseemly, disorderly, and frequently indecent din and cacophony of diverse communities of faith, speaking of and about God and speaking to and against and past one another, is the sign of the truth of who God is and what church is? What if?

Eberhard Jüngel, in his brief commentary on the Theological Declaration of Barmen, inquires specifically into "the theological criteria which operate in relation to our God-talk within the Christian faith."[19] In a manner reminiscent of Calvin, Jüngel recognizes the situation of the church in the ambiguity of its creaturely existence, which we commonly designate as "culture." The divine counterpoint to this "inevitable ambivalence and ambiguity" is not an idealized church but the reign of God over all life. The church's role is to remind (under Word and Sacrament) the human polis of the meaning of God's reign of divine justice and peace, wisdom and love, "which makes everything unambiguous."[20]

How, we might ask, does God's reign make everything unambiguous?—especially when we remember the Pauline comment that became crucial to the Reformers: "Christ has become wisdom for us" (I Corinthians 1:30).[21] Jesus Christ is our wisdom, peace, love, and justice. God's reign is not a simple declarative statement, a command or a law, but is the incarnate Word; the eternal utterance plunged headlong into human society, flesh and blood, the matrix of culture. John Calvin in his discussion of church suggests that the uncertain and insecure nature of the human community of faith is crucial to its identity; these people in their faith in God through Jesus Christ ultimately have no one else to cling to.[22] This is the character of

God's claim, yet it cannot be heard as divine claim apart from the ambiguity of human community and speech—in the concrete expressions of communities of faith. Amid the "inevitable ambivalence and ambiguity" of human culture, this un-ambiguous claim that cannot merely be codified must be trusted and therefore known in and through communities of faith, that is, through the continuing *kenosis* of God's Word through the power of God's Spirit, in God's vulnerable and con-temporaneous act of self-giving to the church in the particularity of human cul-tures. Our words cling to the Word. We believe this.

Minding the Church

T. E. Peck lectured to his students in 1880:

> [T]he church is the great and last result contemplated by the revelation con-cerning God, man and salvation. . . . She is not only the object of the work-ing of that Triune God of whom theology treats, and the subject of that sin and salvation of which anthropology and soteriology treat, but to her have been committed the lively oracles which alone determine the faith of man-kind upon these classes of truths, and through her are these truths to be pub-lished to the race. The contents of the message are to be pondered first, then the nature of the messenger. This is the rational order.[23]

Is this the rational order? *Must* we (indeed, *can* we) ponder first the "contents of the message" and only subsequently consider the historical situation (or, as Peck has it, abstractly, "nature"?) of the communities that gave rise to the message? Of course, Peck does not believe the communities gave rise to the message at all, but that the message (singular) dropped out of heaven upon the church.

Is it possible to speak of "church" abstractly? Yes, of course it is possible. Peck is capable of drumming out over two hundred closely printed pages that define "church" according to abstract "principles."[24] But if we speak in this manner are we describing "church" that occurs anywhere except in someone's mind as a sort of ide-alized essence? Are we, in other words, describing a church that has never existed?

One way of getting at these questions is to ask another: What church is Peck de-scribing? The church he describes is, he tells us, a society made up of adhering indi-viduals or individuals who are brought into this society by those who will vouch for them. And so Peck says that while it is strictly true "that a man becomes a Christian and a member of the church at the same time by the same act of God," nevertheless "in the order of nature he must become a Christian first."[25] The church as society is voluntary. It is an aggregate of adherents. It is therefore characterized by adult mem-bers who are able to make "credible" confessions of faith and holiness as terms of membership and communion and infants of these members who are recognized as members in a manner analogous to minors in a civil society.[26] The church of which Peck speaks is characterized by "certain sacred rites and forms of worship through which this credible profession is made, and the covenant state of infants recognized" and "a certain 'order' of government, or system of discipline, in the hands of church officers, called of God and chosen by the people."[27] Church, he continues, is characterized by "the possession and use of oracles, ministry, ordinances, for the ingathering of the elect and their sanctification; in other words, for the completion of the mystical body of Christ, the church invisible"; it is further characterized by its adherence to catholicity and the spiritual unity of the church throughout the world.[28]

Peck's language about church distinguishes the church of which he speaks as Protestant and North American; his references to the seventeenth-century Westminster standards of faith and to Hermann Witsius and Francis Turretin (among other authorities) places his church generally in the Reformed family, and particularly in the Presbyterian camp, in his case, in its southern American branch. Peck, however, does not wish to recognize these signs of particularity specifically as signs of particularity; as such they are largely irrelevant to him. What he indicates is that "church" (true, essential Church) is distinguished by these very things that one can clearly mark out as particular and peculiar to his community's understanding of itself. My purpose is not to pick on Professor Peck. He does what one frequently does when one is bent on essentialism in ecclesiology: He merely imagines that his own signs of particularity point to essence (marks of the true church) while at the same time imagining that another's signs of particularity indicate inauthenticity.

The question that presses itself upon us in light of such an approach is this: <u>Is it possible to speak of "church" by reveling in the signs of particularity in various communities of faith and by recognizing in their use the communities of faith that worship God and live together historically</u>? If we are able to speak of church in this manner, then perhaps we can move beyond the uninteresting question of essence (What is "church"? What are the qualities of "churchness"?) to some really interesting questions. For example: What is being said *here* in this service of worship or *there* in that act of ministry? How do these people understand as statements of faith the actions involved in burying their dead? What is meant by this word or sign or gesture or symbol when it is used in this way? The diversity of communities of faith is not a theme in search of unity; it is what it is, at the call of the incarnate God. Our goal, therefore, is, as Roland Barthes suggests, not to discern beneath "this pluralism a type of unity . . . magically produced"[29] but to enjoy the pluralism iself, as we might add, as an engagement with God and God's people in their communities of faith—where they are.

In this context Barthes's critique of "this ambiguous myth of human 'community'" is especially pertinent. He criticizes an exhibition in France that was titled "The Great Family of Man," in which human cultures were presented as possessing a core of common experiences, as follows:

> [M]an is born, works, laughs and dies everywhere in the same way; and if there still remains in these acts some ethnic peculiarity, at least one hints that

there is underlying each one an identical "nature," that their diversity is only formal and does not belie the existence of a common mould.[30]

Human beings are thus removed from their historical particularity, are abstracted from that which is truly human, their cultural concreteness; and their behaviors are "moralized and sentimentalized" into a "great family" symbolism to serve the ideology of humanism. "But if one removed History from them, there is nothing more to be said about them; any comment about them becomes purely tautological."[31] Birth and death, for instance, mean nothing as universally human experiences or ideas. Rather—

> [W]hat does the "essence" of this process matter to us, compared to its modes which, as for them, are perfectly historical? Whether or not the child is born with ease or difficulty, whether or not his birth causes suffering to his mother, whether or not he is threatened by a high mortality rate, whether or not such and such a type of future is open to him: this is what your Exhibitions should be telling people, instead of an eternal lyricism of birth. The same goes for death: must we really celebrate its essence once more, and thus risk forgetting that there is still so much we can do to fight it?[32]

Uttering "the church" as an abstract concept tells us little about the church we inhabit—even if we intone the words in a properly modulated ecclesiastical voice. What tells us something worth investigating is the discovery of how a community of faith understands itself as church, how it functions under the signs of its own particularity, how congregants use the vocabulary of their faith to make sense of life or attempt to understand what happens in their worship when a person is baptized or the Eucharistic meal is shared or preaching is heard or feet are washed. And to speak in this manner of particularity does not imply that "particular" is merely a synonym for local, parochial, or provincial; "particular" can express broader peculiarities, that which is peculiar to an ethnic or national or confessional expression of Christian community as well as that which is locally particular to a Baptist congregation in western Tennessee; it can express certain aspects of, for instance, Roman Catholicism, or Roman Catholicism in Brazil, or Swedish-American Lutheranism. What is being said, in a manner analogous to Barthes's comments (to reproduce—photographically—"death or birth tells us, literally, nothing"), is this: An abstract concept does not grant access to existence. It is purely self-referential and therefore tautological. Existence must be penetrated horizontally as history. And it is there, in their use, that we understand the meaning of the words we employ.

So it is that we understand the meaning of church in our use of the word in historical particularity. This is why Jesus of Nazareth, whom we believe to be the Christ, is irreducible in his historical existence (his humanity is particular, not universal) and why his birth, his life, ministry, teachings, cross, and Resurrection as the signs of particularity are also irreducible (they are grounded in a particular time and place), why the Church at Corinth or Ephesus or Alexandria or Rome is church not ideally, but *there,* and why essential "churchness" is unworthy of our seeking while "church" is essential to our life of faith.

OF AIRPORTS AND THE EIFFEL TOWER

One of the most popular essays by Roland Barthes concerns the way the Eiffel Tower functions as a kind of complex sign. I was recently rereading this essay while waiting for a plane, when a woman sat down next to me. Out of the corner of my eye I could see her scanning the cover of the book, which bears the title The Eiffel Tower and Other Mythologies.[33]

She asked, "How can the Eiffel Tower be a mythology? It really exists! It's not a myth!"

I am an introvert and I do not ordinarily seek out conversation with strangers, so my natural inclination is not to respond to such queries as cordially as one might desire. But my curiosity overruled my irritation. I responded.

"Barthes is not using the word mythology to indicate that something does not exist or that it is fanciful, but that a variety of meanings are attached to it. He is saying that the Eiffel Tower functions as a kind of cultural sign. It communicates certain things by its very existence. Meanings and significance and values are attached to it. Thus the Eiffel Tower, while it is an architectural structure, functions as a myth."

I am not sure if her next response was a base attempt at flattery or just wide of the mark.

She asked, "And what is your major young man?" Ours is a university town, so I thought I would interpret this as favorably as possible.

I answered, "Actually I'm not a student. I am a seminary professor."

A look of pure puzzlement crossed her face. She started to speak. Then halted herself. Then began again. "But what does this have to do with religion?"

I said, "I teach about the church. I am investigating what it might mean for the church to function as a sign."

"But the church is just the church," she said.

Now, I want to leave to one side the question which Barthes touches on concerning the insecurity of the bourgeoisie, which leads us, because of our desire to maintain the illusion of a controllable, predictable universe of meaning, to reduce all knowledge to tautology; the common bourgeois fear is that something will surprise us by meaning something (ironically, paradoxically, or dialectically) we do not expect it to mean. I want to focus instead on the *puzzlement* at the idea that the church could mean something, could "stand" for something or signify something, in its existence as church, that is, that the church functions as a sign.

Barthes discusses the manner in which the Eiffel Tower offers the "reader" a symbol of Paris and of France and of all things French, a symbol so clearly recognizable that its silhouette can be attached to all sorts of scenes on tourist brochures and posters to identify them immediately as Gallic: "This is a French scene," says the silhouette. "You are looking at a picture of France." This is clearly communicated by the sign of the tower, even if you are only looking at a photograph of two children embracing on a street corner (they could be children of any nationality on any street corner) or a landscape that could as easily be Swiss or Belgian.

The image of the tower can stand in — in a sort of representational substitution — for cultural or national values, depending on the context in which we see it and what readership views it. Barthes points out that the tower is a virtually empty sign, a pure signifier, that is, "a form" into which or upon which people can unceasingly place meaning, *because it means everything*.[34] "Who can say what the Tower will be for humanity tomorrow?" he asks. Our knowledge and experience, dreams, aspirations and history, our greed and narrowness, all that we are and do shapes our attachment to this sign, and the content we attach to it. It can symbolize resistence to tyrany or complicity with evil, political shrewdness or naiveté, high culture or low; the list of past, present, and future possibilities is virtually endless. Barthes continues, "there can be no doubt it will always be something, and something of humanity itself. Glance, object, symbol, such is the infinite circuit of functions which permits it always to be something other and something much more than the Eiffel Tower."[35]

In the beginning, as the construction of the tower was rationalized, its architect, Gustave Eiffel, defended the project by explaining how "useful" the tower would be for the advancement of science and medicine.[36] Of course, there is no convincing utilitarian justification for the tower. It does not now exist for any "useful" purpose. It exists as a sign. It functions to sign. People do not visit it to learn something from it. They visit it merely to see it, to be there. And, in this, paradoxically, they are betrayed by the sign. Because to see the tower is immediately to see through it. The tower has no cultural "inner life." It does not contain artifacts or works of art. It contains only meaning, the meaning attached to it. The tower can, however, function as a place from which to see other things. It is an observatory. Barthes alludes to Maupassant who lunched regularly at the restaurant in the tower, not because he enjoyed the food but because it was the only place in Paris where he didn't have to look at the tower.[37] But from the tower (the sign functioning as observatory), one sees Paris; and one sees Paris from a perspective at once immanent and transcendent. The intimacy of the view from the tower is startling. One may observe a pair of lovers quarreling or a worker at lunch reading a newspaper. But one cannot hear the lovers' discourse or speak to the reader. If this is the God's-eye view, then it must be admitted that intimacy is impaired by a certain dubious advantage of perspective. We can look over only by being left out.

Barthes asks, finally, "[W]hy do we visit the Eiffel Tower?" He answers, "No doubt in order to participate in a dream of which it is (and this is its originality) much more the crystallizer than the true object."[38] The tower's function as sign attracts us to that which transcends it. Even to look out from the tower is to transcend the tower, is to participate in an archaeology of the mythology of Paris, of France and humanity.

I wonder what it might mean for us to inquire into the significance of the church by asking, literally, what does it mean to understand the church itself as a sign? This is not a new question. Cyprian, the third-century bishop and martyr, understood the church's unity as a representation, a sign, of the oneness of Christ and the oneness of God.[39] Martin Luther regarded the church, inasmuch as it bears witness to Jesus Christ (the one true sacrament of God), as bearing *signa sacramentalia* (sacramental signs), that is, signs that point toward the act of God on behalf of humanity.[40]

Eberhard Jüngel perceptively places the center of gravity of this sign in the total being of the church as the recipient of God's grace. The church is the sign that says who God is by its utter reliance, its trustful dependence, upon Jesus Christ. Drawing on Luther's sermon on Matthew 28, in which Luther says, "There is no greater sinner than the Christian church," Jüngel says: "We should note carefully that he does not consider the church's existence as the 'greatest sinner' to stand in contradiction to its existence as the one, *holy,* catholic and apostolic church; rather, it is a proof of the church's holiness."[41] This gathering of sinners—which the church is (casta meretrix, "pure harlot")—bears witness to the one who forgives.

> It is precisely through the church's understanding of itself as *peccatrix maxima* [the greatest sinner] that the intimate relation between the church and Jesus Christ is expressed. And thereby Jesus Christ is taken seriously as the Son of God who in his holiness is not simply concerned with 'his own person' but with 'all sinners so that in the power of his holiness he became 'a sinner of sinners'. His holiness, because it is a holiness which takes pity on sinners, makes him into a *peccator peccatorum* [sinner of sinners] in their place; the holiness of the church, on the other hand, leads it to recognize itself as *peccatrix maxima.* As the *peccator peccatorum,* Christ is holy because he wipes away our sins, whereas as the *peccatrix maxima* the holy church remains ever dependent upon the fact that its sins have been wiped away. He is the sacrament which the church receives, to which the church can only testify and which the church must hand on as a recipient. And so prayer for the forgiveness of its own sins is the criterion by which we decide whether, in representing and presenting the sacramental event, 'mother church' understands itself *secundum dicentem deum* [as speaking what God speaks] or whether it misunderstands itself as self-representation.[42]

Protestant theologians have been hesitant to speak of the church as sign, Jüngel observes, because of their appropriate concern about idolatry, confusing the creature with the Creator or blurring the line between humanity and God, and because of a corresponding protestation against the tyranny of salvation by works (the threat of which Jüngel discerns within the various self-realization and self-fulfillment movements in contemporary society). Protestant theology has tended to speak of the tension between the Word of God and the community of faith, seeing God's self-disclosure through the Word as the event that surprises and calls into question the human gathering (church), at the same time that the Word offers the grace and forgiveness of God, which can only be received. Inasmuch as this corrective counters human attempts to equate our ways with God's ways, it is of course valuable and necessary. From this perspective it is essential to say that the church functions as a sign inasmuch as it points away from itself toward the holy God who in Jesus Christ forgives humanity in general and, in particular, the community that gathers in conscious awareness and in faith to hear God's Word of forgiveness.

However, is there not something more at stake in recognizing the church's status as sign? Does the church not, in its reliance upon the Spirit of God, in its hearing of the Word of God, point in faith to God in Jesus Christ *in its participation in the life of God,* in its integration as a community of faith, in its constitution as humanity in relationship, in its communion in and through the life of the triune God? In other words, is it not true that our very being in communion points as a sign to the God whose being is in communion?[43] Is there not a real participation in the life of the ascended Christ, the heavenly High Priest, through his Spirit? And is this participation not a sharing in the body and blood of Christ in such a way that the life of the church—the existence of gathered communities in worship and their dispersion into the world—functions as a sign of Jesus Christ? The church as sign cannot merely point to or signify itself (self-representation) without losing its existence as sign. But the church's existence as sign conveys more than justification; the church signals God's continuing priestly event of sharing God's own life with humanity. Participation in the life of God is no less the act of God than justification; receiving the grace of God is no more an act of reception than is "living by the Spirit."

The church is the sign of the grace of God in that it demonstrates God's grace, God's love, God's utter vulnerability in God's self-giving on behalf of and for the other, for a world in rebellion against God, for a God-amnesiacal world, a world that in receiving God betrays and in bearing witness also denies God. Thus, the sign of the church is always the sign of the cross as that which the world committed against God, that which God suffered willingly at the hands of the world, that which God allows to stand to demonstrate God's love toward the world, that which the world itself suffers at its own hands, and that which the church suffers in relation to the world to which it belongs in obedience to the God to whom it belongs even more surely and absolutely. The church, therefore, as Jüngel observes, "is the analogate which points to Jesus Christ as the analogue. As analogue, the church reveals that Jesus Christ himself is the one who brings men and women into correspondence with himself as the church. And so we may—with Schleiermacher—speak of a self-representation of Jesus Christ occurring in the actions of the church." The church, then is, again as Jüngel says, "the great *sacramental sign* which represents Jesus Christ."[44]

Practically speaking, this means that the church in its historical concreteness functions as a gesture and a signal pointing toward Jesus Christ by doing what it ordinarily does and being what it ordinarily is: the proclaimer and audience of the Word of God, the theater of the various acts of the Holy Spirit. The church is sign of God in its flesh and blood reality as Corpus Christi, as communities, as gatherings, as communion in these common elements that are always human, creaturely, sinful, yet holy in the hands of the holy God. The church is at once the sign outside the church building, telling us to whom the church belongs even while it points to the most distinctively human features of the church, and the house—*oikas*—the household of faith itself. "St. Thomas More," "Trinity Presbyterian Church," "St. Michael and All Angels Anglican Church," "First Assembly of God," "The Church of Christ Meets Here"—even when the sign lies "Westminster Abbey" (the abbey to which it points is long-gone) we get the message. Under and in and through this sign we know God. And this is, itself, the *musterion,* is it not? This is, itself, the bearing witness, the *re*presenting and *pre*senting of the sacrament of God, the sign of the incarnation, the incarnation that is Jesus Christ, Emmanuel; the church is the sign that endures in its fragile humanity because it does not endure in its own power but endures precisely in the power of an-Other, the one whose name consists in not being named. And from this vantage point, from under, within and through this sign, we at last see and know—*God.*

5

Confessions

A Preface to Ecclesiology

Confessional Questions

On the sixteenth of April 1963, a young clergyman sat in the Birmingham, Alabama, city jail. He was there for leading a civil rights demonstration. As he sat in the cell that day, he wrote a letter that stands beside the Declaration of Independence, the Federalist Papers, and Lincoln's Gettysburg Address as one of a handful of American documents that define and call into question our national character. The document also stands as a remarkable example of Christian theological reflection. The young minister: Martin Luther King, Jr. The document: the "Letter from Birmingham City Jail." He wrote the letter in response to an open letter, published the previous January, from eight leading white "liberal" clergymen, all from Alabama, who charged King's civil rights efforts with being "unwise and untimely." There is an especially haunting passage in King's letter that specifically pertains to our quest to understand how we go about describing church. It presses us as church to a position that simultaneously "confesses" both in the sense of a confession of sin and in the sense of a confession of faith. The passage reads:

> I have traveled the length and breadth of Alabama, Mississippi and all the other Southern states. On sweltering summer days and crisp autumn mornings I have looked at her beautiful churches with their spires pointing heavenward. I have beheld the impressive outlay of her massive religious education buildings. Over and over again I have found myself asking: "Who worships here? Who is their God?"[1]

Like a skilled surgeon, King probed the open wound in white churches in the American South. He questioned its members' theological ethics, which separated flesh and spirit in a docetic ecclesiology of social convenience. Shut out by the power structures of the white elite, the ruling class—members of which worshiped under the sign of those "spires pointing heavenward"—King asked Where was the voice of the white church when Governors Barnett and Wallace reinforced the hatred and prejudice of their exclusive social power structures? "Where," King asked, "were their voices of support when tired, bruised, and weary Negro men and women decided to rise from the dark dungeons of complacency to the bright hills of creative protest?" Anticipating those who might object to his criticism of the church, who might be offended by his disparaging tone in speaking of church, the holy and spiritual communion, King continued by saying, "Yes, I see the church as the body of Christ. But, oh! How we have blemished and scarred that body through social neglect and fear of being nonconformists."[2]

King's questions open the way for us to go about our task of describing church, of doing theological reflection on the church, in the church, and through the church in the face of death. King's questions insist that we must understand who we are in relationship to who we believe God to be, that our conception of *God's character* profoundly relates to the question of *our character*, that both are grounded in the reality of our particular social contexts and that each shapes our shaping of all our theological, ecclesiastical, social, and political endeavors.

King's questions anchor us in the actuality of human social engagements and will not permit us to float off into abstractions that begin with the phrase "Well, *ideally* the church should . . ." King stands in our way and will not permit us easily to walk the path that harkens back to the classical misperceptions of Cyprian, Augustine, and the Alexandrian school of ecclesiology, whose Platonic dichotomy between the visible and invisible church separated for centuries the church's "is" from the church's "ought" and has continued in this century to justify injustice in the minds of many women and men of the church and to make it more likely that Christians will retreat into crystal clear religious abstractions for fear of confronting ambiguous reality under the sovereign reign of God.

King's questions particularly resonate with those of us in the Reformed tradition, echoing John Calvin's call to an epistemology that springs from the knowledge of God and of ourselves as "joined," Calvin says, by so many bonds that it is difficult to discern "which one precedes and brings forth the other."[3] Ludwig Wittgenstein describes the problem with the kind of knowledge that Calvin speaks of and King's questions call for. Often the thing that "makes a subject hard to understand," writes Wittgenstein, especially if that subject is "something significant and important—is not that before you can understand it you need to be specially trained in abstruse matters." In other words, it is not technical information or expert status that stands between us and knowledge. Rather, that which makes knowledge difficult is "the contrast between understanding the subject and what most people *want* to see. Because of this the very things which are most obvious may become the hardest of all to understand. What has to be overcome is a difficulty having to do with the will, rather than with the intellect."[4]

As a reader of Calvin's *Institutes* quickly discerns, the barrier to knowledge of God and ourselves is not our lack of technical information or the data available to a closed expert class but the various filters that our own pride and unwillingness to deal with the implications of our understanding place between our understanding and what really exists. King certainly implies this in his questions, especially in reference to our knowledge of the church. Both King and Calvin call for an engagement with the reality of the church that ordinarily lies in our path rather than with an imaginary, idealistic church that exists only in abstract ratiocination—an engagement that requires of us what G. K. Chesterton once described as that most soaring variety of imagination, the imagination to see what is really there.[5] What we require, then, is the imagination to speak clearly about what it means when we speak of the church ordinarily.

Again, let us return to King's questions. King traversed the American South in those days when Jim Crow laws reigned supreme, unable to sleep in motels that were reserved for white clientele, unable to drink from the cool water fountains reserved for the lips of white people, unable to eat at lunch counters reserved for white diners, unable to use toilet facilities reserved for white customers. King noticed—not merely coincidentally—that white church members owned those businesses, ran those towns, enforced those laws, and worshiped and sang praises to God and studied the Bible in those churches whose dreaming spires reached toward heaven. And out of the pain of exclusion King was compelled to ask, Who worships in these white churches? Who is the God being worshiped? His holy and prophetic grief gave utterance to a linguistic theophany, interrogating the church, demanding that our speech about church in this world correspond with our speech about church as eternal.

King's questions require and evoke a quality of theological reflection that to one degree or another has always taken place in the church, though pride and self-interest have at times compromised the integrity of that reflection. Karl Barth at seventy described well the quality of theological reflection for which King argued: "Theology requires free men. . . . A good theologian does not live in a house of ideas, principles and methods. He walks right through all such buildings and always comes out into the fresh air again."[6] To speak of theology as primarily a task performed by "free" persons "in the fresh air" and not primarily as a matter performed in the closed house of "ideas, principles and methods"—to speak of theology as a task performed (in King's words) traveling along city streets "on sweltering summer days and crisp autumn mornings"—is to say that theology is primarily a way of paying attention to the particularity of our creaturely, our human, existence, to understand that existence in the consciousness of God's presence, and to articulate our relationship to the sovereign reign of God over all creation in Jesus Christ.

Søren Kierkegaard wrote (with beguiling understatement): "Christianity's claim that it had come into the world by a beginning that was simultaneously historical and eternal had caused philosophy much difficulty."[7] Certainly every utterance we make regarding church touches this difficulty. The problem of speaking a theological word that claims to be true is irrevocably linked to the crisis of history and eternity that is inextricably bound up with Christian faith as faith in Jesus of Nazareth in whom we believe we have encountered the eternal God, immortal, invisible, only wise. Despite the paradox, our vocation as followers of Jesus Christ compels us to speak theological words that aspire to truth.[8] In other words, as Reinhold Niebuhr observed, as Christians we exist as citizens of two worlds. We can hardly afford to renounce our citizenship in either the eternal realm or the historical.[9] But between these two realms there is fixed a boundary, a chasm, an ugly ditch over which we believe we can pass but once and cannot return, and this fact underlies and undercuts every word we have to speak about God and our loyalty to God's reign. We are forbidden to speak beyond this boundary; yet we are compelled to do precisely this. This quandary represents, to a large degree, who we are as Christians.

To understand our life as church, then — specifically attempting in our churchly settings to answer the questions of worship and identity posed by King — we cannot afford to ignore what it means to live on the boundary between eternity and history or (perhaps more accurately) what it means to live immersed in the particularity of history under the reign of the eternal God who became flesh and dwelt among us in Jesus Christ. As people who believe in the God who did not abhor the Virgin's womb, we make a startling claim (a shocking, a "scandalous" claim, according to Saint Paul): God is known in particularity. God became human. The Creator became a creature. The Word became flesh. The Truth (mysterious, inaccessible, eternal, and immutable) became a fact (observable, contingent, and changeable) among other historical facts.[10] Thus, again, we must speak of death, that is, if we are to speak of incarnation appropriately, because death marks the boundary. The death of Jesus Christ is contained in his birth. Indeed, his birth is a kind of death, a death to the otherworldliness of deity that utterly transforms our understanding of transcendence.[11] Robert Frost wrote: "Pulpiteers will censure / Our instinctive venture / Into what they call / The material / When we took the fall / From the apple tree. / But God's own descent / Into flesh was meant / As a demonstration / That the supreme merit / Lay in risking spirit / In substantiation."[12] We can never again look at barns with quite the same expectation, knowing that God made God's appearing in one; nor can we gaze upon trees with theological disinterest, realizing that God was put to death on one; water speaks of death as well as life, and bread and wine nourish by drawing us into this community that lives perennially *zwischen den Zeiten* and belonging more to the eschatological future than to the past. History cannot remain for us only a dull and monotonous round of birth and death, of nations rising against nations and of political intramural scrimmages that characterize the ways and means of the world at large, because God chose to enter into history and to make creaturely existence the theater of redemption.

This is why Barth could not live closed up in a house of "ideas, principles and methods." This is why King's questions represent more than a political challenge to social power structures. God in Christ lays claim to the world, this world, and not some other. If we aspire to know God we must know God amid, and in, and through, and not despite, the ambiguities and contingencies of historical existence (and even "existence" must be carefully qualified here to protest against any interpretation that would remove the plurality from it; "existence" is not a back door through which "being" can sneak). We do not, with Platonism, seek the eternal ideals beyond the material; nor, with Husserl's phenomenology, do we seek the pure, universal, or essential thing itself beyond the flux of contextual experiences. We seek, rather, to hear and bear witness to Christ Jesus who calls us to follow in and through the radical and frequently embarrassing particularity, the flux and ambiguity, contingency and ambivalence of creaturely existence.[13]

To speak of the church, we do not remove ourselves to abstractions but climb into an automobile beside a young clergyman who at the risk of his own life crisscrossed the American South attempting to help people liberate themselves; and as we look at the churches along our way with their tall spires and impressive Christian education buildings we must ask with him: "Who worships here? Who is their God?" To speak of the church, we walk out into the fresh air of humanity; we refuse to sit at narrow desks in the cramped countinghouse of ideals and idealism; and we must ask with Karl Barth and others: What does it mean to hear, to trust, and obey Jesus Christ as the Word of God in life and in death?

To speak of the church, in fact, we begin in the dwelling place of our habitation, attempting to discern God in the midst of the worshiping congregations we know most intimately, paying attention to the sacred texts and confessional statements that we hear and believe in worship and study in a variety of settings throughout and among the congregational fellowships we indwell, paying close attention to the living texts of the people of God in the ambiguity of the lives we live under the unambiguous claim of God's reign.[14] Only by doing so can we discern that we do not need to change our addresses in order to dwell in the house of the Lord.

CONFESSIONAL METHODS

One of the most striking features of the theologies of Basil of Caesarea, Gregory of Nazianzus, Cyril of Jerusalem, John Chrysostom, Augustine of Hippo, Bernard of Clairvaux, Martin Luther, John Calvin, Jonathan Edwards, Friederich Schleiermacher, Karl Barth, Dietrich Bonhoeffer, and Reinhold Niebuhr (among many others) is that they wrote not systematic theology but reflective and occasional theology, that is, theological reflection on matters at hand. Indeed, so-called classical theology, far from being systematic, remains practical. The immediate and ordinary "practice" of the church seeks to understand who the church is and what the church is doing by reflecting on the theological significance of its statements and actions.[15] Rather than being a mere recital of the "history of what theologians have thought," theology classically springs from the matrix of contemporary experiences and churchly practice and represents a profound and ecclesial[16] immediacy of theological reflection on human existence as the life of faith in the God revealed in Jesus Christ.[17]

When one thinks of Chrysostom one is reminded, for instance, of sermons.

When one recalls Cyril of Jerusalem one thinks of catechetical lectures. When one reflects on Gregory of Nyssa, Gregory of Nazianzus, and Basil of Caesarea (the three giants of Cappadocia) one's mind turns to letters, orations, and homilies.

Augustine of Hippo, arguably the greatest theologian of the ancient church, was first and foremost an occasional theologian (that is, a theologian who responds to issues, concerns, and situations that arise in a social context); indeed Augustine was in his own way as much an occasional theologian as Karl Rahner[18] or Paula Cooey.[19] His *Confessions* speaks the language of a pilgrim's journal. The *City of God* practices apologetics. One should understand even the majestic *Christian Doctrine* primarily as a homiletical endeavor.

When we consider it as a whole, John Calvin's corpus is dominated by his sermons and commentaries on Scripture, which represent an astonishing reading of biblical texts (one book after another) in relation to the currents and daily concerns of the church's life in his particular social and historical context. Calvin's *Institutes* (edition following edition, from 1536 to 1559) serve no less lively and topical interests than his occasional writings in response to various crises and concerns in church and society (such as his brilliant reply to Cardinal Sadolet's letter to the senate and people of Geneva).[20]

Despite the subtleties of Karl Barth's *Church Dogmatics*, the attentive student of this massive work discerns neither a theological "system" nor an idealistic exercise in theoretical aesthetics but an elaborate tapestry of churchly reflections on the relationship between God and creation, a weaving that, however intellectually beautiful, intricate, and elastic, never removes itself from the actual daily lives and concerns of communities of faith in the larger context of human society and politics.

If one hopes to describe the life, the faith and ministry, of the church, then one must recognize that our task requires simultaneous attentiveness to two realities: (1) the reality of the God in whose image (Father, Son, and Holy Spirit) we are created, whose Spirit and Word constitute our being-in-communion as humans and as Body of Christ; and (2) the context of communities of faith among the realities in which we live, worship, and are concretely constituted as people of God in and for the sake of God's world.

The question of how to live attentive to God and human communities of faith in the world raises the familiar question of theological method. In order to carry out this dual task, in reference to the development of ecclesiology, one might be tempted to describe the theological consideration of the church as *ecclesiology from below* and *ecclesiology from above* in a manner parallel to that in which dogmatic theology has dealt with Christology. I shall explore this approach briefly; then, in rejecting this approach, I shall propose an alternative.

In christological studies, "Christology from above" refers to a deductive method of dealing with the question, Who is Jesus Christ? As George Hendry observed, a Christology from above "began from the eternal Godhead of the Son (as that was established in the doctrine of the Trinity), then went on to speak of the incarnation and the humanity of the incarnate God. In so doing it faithfully reflects and celebrates the downward movement of the grace of God in his condescension to us."[21] One finds some notable examples of this approach to Christology in sources as varied as Athanasius, the fourth-century champion of orthodoxy, the Westminster standards of the seventeenth century, and in recent years in the dogmatic theology of Thomas F. Torrance.[22] One cannot deny the beauty and coherence of this theological approach. "But," again as Hendry has written, it can at times obscure "the fact that we know God only as we encounter his presence in Christ here below."[23]

There exists, as already indicated, a corresponding "ecclesiology from above." It proceeds also in a deductive movement, reflecting on what it might mean to describe the church as the Body of Christ or a People of God. It takes great care to construct from his perspective a cogent and coherent description of the church as a spiritual reality the existence of which one can only apprehend by faith. This approach guards against any reduction of the divine givenness of the church, the church *as* God's gift of grace.

In christological studies, the contrasting "Christology from below" refers to an inductive method that maintains (in the words of Emil Brunner) that "the way to the knowledge of Jesus leads from the human Jesus to the Son of God and to the Godhead.... It is the miracle of the divine condescension towards us that He wills to meet us in a human being. If *God* has opened this way to Himself for us, we ought to follow it too; we have no right to try to reverse the process."[24] This christological perspective is enriched especially by the *theologia crucis* of Protestant Reformer Martin Luther and also by Peter Taylor Forsyth and Jürgen Moltmann.[25]

Certain expressions of "Christology from below" contribute to a reductionism in regard to the person of Jesus Christ, however. The nineteenth-century quest for the historical Jesus and the popular work of some participants in the current Jesus Seminar especially demonstrate this. Their indulgence in a simplistic opposition of the Jesus of history to the Christ of faith fails to comprehend the crucial theological point of the gospels as canonical documents: There is, for the church, no remembrance and no understanding of Jesus except as the Christ. Recent scholarly attempts to gain access to a Jesus prior to or apart from Jesus Christ flounder in romantic interpretations both of God's relationship to history and the church's political/theological reality in the world, which is to say, they have predictably weak or nonexistent pneumatologies and ecclesiologies, in addition to the problems they have with regard to Christology.

In many ways similar dangers of reductionism lurk within an "ecclesiology from below." Such approaches to the church tend to regard the church merely as a form of social grouping, a phenomenon fully describable in sociological and anthropological, ethnographic and psychological terms. This approach sometimes even views "faith" as a retreat in the face of reason and experience, discounting the idea that the church is somehow more than can be defined in what we commonly call scientific, empirical, or historical terms.

In contrast to these approaches to ecclesiology that envision two separate movements of conceptualizing the church "from above" or "from below"—as though the church exists as two separate entities or realities—Edward Schillebeeckx offers an alternative. He proposes that we understand the church as a "single reality." He writes:

> We are always concerned with one and the same reality: the form which has grown up through history and which can be explained sociologically or historically . . . is precisely what the believer experiences and expresses in the language of faith as a specific manifestation of grace: a successful, less successful or improper response of the believing community to God's grace. There is no "surplus of revelation" behind or above the socio-historical forms of ministry. . . . Although it transcends the forms in which it is expressed, grace can only be found *in* the historical or sociological form, not beyond it or above it.[26]

In Schillebeeckx's approach, we are asked to conceive of the church in what one might describe as an "incarnational paradigm." We find a parallel to this alternative ecclesiology also in the study of Christology, this time in the approach of Dietrich Bonhoeffer.

Bonhoeffer explains that above all else, Christology cannot become a matter of merely classifying Jesus within already existing patterns and categories of existence, asking the question, How?[27] (How is this possible? How can Jesus Christ be both human and divine?) Our existing patterns and categories cannot make sense of Jesus Christ because he is God in the flesh, the unique and unprecedented possibility of God unknown to all prior human experiences and possibilities. The Word made flesh is the limit against which our human languages meet their ultimate limitation. This divine Reason forms the boundary of our rational powers, a boundary as final, as irreducible, as irrevocable as death. Our words are relativized, shattered, and left to stand in stunned silence before this Word.[28] "To speak of Christ, then," Bonhoeffer writes, "will be to speak within the context of the silence of the church. We must study christology in the humble silence of the worshiping community. Prayer is to be silent and cry out at the same time, before God in the presence of his Word. We have come together as a community to study Christ, God's Word."[29]

Bonhoeffer continues by explaining how it is in the presence of Jesus Christ.

> There is in fact only one question left: "Who are you? Speak!" The question "Who are you?" is the question of deposed, distraught reason. But it is equally the question of faith: Who are you? Are you God himself? This is the question with which christology is concerned. Christ is the Anti-Logos. There is no longer any possibility of classification because the existence of this Logos means the end of the human Logos. The question "Who are you?" is the only appropriate question. To this question the phenomenon discloses itself. Christ gives an answer to the question "Who?"[30]

According to Bonhoeffer, when we are confronted by Jesus Christ we are confronted by that reality that calls reality into question. We are confronted in Jesus Christ by the final boundary, the Word that renders words silent, the silence of the grave, or the silence of faith that points to the possibility beyond the grave. We are compelled by our existence to ask, Who are you? We stand within our particular existence with this question on our lips, asking the question of our existence *toward* the boundary. This is the question of transcendence, but a fully immanent transcendence, a transcendence embedded in and pervading human community. We inquire "about the being which is alien to" our own being, "about the boundaries" of our own existence. Bonhoeffer writes that "the question of transcendence is the question of existence and the question of existence is the question of transcendence. In theological terms: man only knows who he is in the light of God."[31]

One may discern in Bonhoeffer's Christology a method at work that bears some similarity to Paul Tillich's "method of correlation, namely the correlation between existential questions and theological answers." Tillich's method is familiar:

The existential question, namely, man himself in the conflicts of his existential situation, is not the source for the revelatory answer formulated by theology. One cannot derive the divine self-manifestation from an analysis of the human predicament. God speaks to the human situation, against it, and for it. . . . Man is the question, not the answer. It is equally wrong to derive the question implied in human existence from the revelatory answer. This is impossible because the revelatory answer is meaningless if there is no question to which it is the answer. Man cannot receive an answer to a question he has not asked. . . . The question, asked by man, is man himself. He asks it, whether or not he is vocal about it. He cannot avoid asking it, because his very being is the question of his existence.[32]

Again, one may discern in Bonhoeffer a parallel between Tillich's method of correlation and Bonhoeffer's discussion of humanity's asking of Christ the "question 'Who?'" However, according to Bonhoeffer, we cannot address this question to Christ in an appropriate manner unless the question has already been answered in an appropriate manner. This means that the question addressed *to* Christ (Who are you?) is posed *by* Christ himself *in* and *on behalf of* humanity, and it is a question that cuts both ways. "It can only be put where the basic presupposition, Christ's claim to be the Logos of God, has been accepted. It can only be put where God is sought because men already know him. There is no general blind seeking after God. Here a man can only seek what has already been found. 'You would not seek me had you not already found me' (Pascal). This idea also occurs in Augustine." Bonhoeffer brings us to the critical, paradoxical point of theological interrogation: "Here, then, is the place at which christology must begin. In the church, in which Christ has revealed himself as the Word of God, the human Logos puts the question: Who are you, Jesus Christ, Word of God, Logos of God? The answer is given, the church receives it new every day. The human Logos seeks to understand it, to ponder it, to explain it."[33]

What is more, the question posed by our existence is, to paraphrase Tillich, humanity itself. In light of Bonhoeffer, even this question is only clearly and appropriately articulated in and by the humanity of Jesus Christ. The incarnation grounds the correlation of God and humanity in the existence of this particular human being, this Palestinian Jew, Jesus of Nazareth, because we believe we are confronted here by the scandal of God's word-act. And because we believe we meet God in *this* human, we believe that our theological reflections cannot seek to deny or avoid the real particularity of human existence(s) in humanity's social-historical concreteness. For Christian communities, on this side of God's continuing incarnation, any word about humanity, any word about God, must pass through this eye of the needle—Jesus Christ.

To describe the church, then, we must attempt to understand it simultaneously from below and above. The church in which Christ reveals himself as Word of God and human Logos is "the called out," "the assembled," "the people of God," "the people of the New Covenant," "the Community of Faith," "the Bride of Christ," "the Body of Christ of which Christ himself is Head," "the Temple of God," broken and triumphant, holy, catholic, and apostolic, *simul iustus et peccator*. The church persists as a sacramental community *and* in various hierarchical forms. It is organic, institutional, and familial. We can describe it in a variety of languages (including sociological and psychological), but we can know it in its totality only through the mystery of faith.[34] To speak pastorally and theologically of the church, one must speak to its identity, must remain focused on the questions provided by Dr. King: Who worships here? Who is their God?[35]

We may follow Hans Urs von Balthasar's example when we speak of the church; we rightly may also ask "*who* is the church?" While von Balthasar's theological approach begins as an "ecclesiology from above," nevertheless we can hold his description of church in tension by focusing on the living organism of the church while pressing home the question of the church's identity as the Body of which Christ is Head. Von Balthasar writes:

> The subject of the Church is, then, simply Christ; he posits and is responsible for her acts in the sense of St. Augustine's reiteration against the Donatists: It is not Peter who baptizes, nor Paul, nor Judas, but Christ alone. . . . The Church . . . is, to use Paul's great simile, *Christ's body*. This means, if we allow its full range of meaning, that the Church, in regard to her Head, is not a person on her own, a new and second one. The "body," in the sense of the simile, forms, together with the "Head," one being, that is, she is a person only "by grace" of the "Head."[36]

While speaking of the church as the Body of Christ, we at the very same time speak of the church, universal and particular, as a social and historical fact among other social and historical facts, as fallen, as a principality and a power among other powers, as a center of political agenda-making and scheming, as a community of human beings fraught with frailty in whom the Spirit of God dwells like a priceless treasure in an earthen vessel. To recognize the facticity, frailty, and fallenness of the church need not take away from the *faith*-full recognition of the church as the Body of Christ (any more than the christological recognition that God was incarnate in our humanity takes away from the wonder of Christ indwelling our actual fallen human flesh). This means: To know the church as the Body of Christ requires us to seek knowledge of it (1) in its actual historical and social existence and (2) by faith in and through Jesus Christ whose Body the church is. One's description of the church *where we find it* must attend to the church's particularity as a creature and (at the same time!) to the Word of God by the power of the Spirit in the church's midst.

CONFESSIONAL FEARS

Our theological descriptions of the church necessarily are attended with irony inasmuch as they remain true to who the church is in its creaturely existence and in its relationship to the God who calls it into existence. Reinhold Niebuhr observed (as I previously noted in another context): "Irony consists of apparently fortuitous incongruities in life which are discovered, upon close examination, to be not merely fortuitous."[37] The ironic situation of the church requires a description of the church that consciously speaks to this irony; the paradoxical character of the church's existence calls for a paradoxically rich ecclesiology. Perhaps nowhere do we see the significance of this ecclesiological irony so well displayed as in Protestant churches in North America who concern themselves with establishing their authentic identity and divine givenness as churches and who struggle within (and attempt to transcend) the creaturely limitations of their historical, social and cultural, ethnic, and economic existence. We can trace the roots of this irony, in part, to the sixteenth-century Reformation of the church, though the roots, in fact, go much deeper; a theological archaeologist would find that this irony resides at the level of the identity of the church. We may rightly predict that, like the poor, this irony will always be (and, indeed, has always been) with us.

John Calvin, discussing the "Holy Catholic Church" in the *Institutes*, seeks to answer the question, "What are the distinguishing marks of the church?" He writes: "We have laid down as distinguishing marks of the church the preaching of the Word and the observance of the sacraments. These can never exist without bringing forth fruit and prospering by God's blessing. I do not say that wherever the Word is preached there will be immediate fruit; but wherever it is received and has a fixed abode, it shows its effectiveness."[38] The Augsburg Confession, of course, lays the groundwork for this distinctively Protestant conception of the church: "For it is sufficient for the true unity of the Christian church that the Gospel be preached in conformity with a pure understanding of it and that the sacraments be administered in accordance with the divine Word."[39] God, through the Word of God, calls the church into being by the power of the Spirit and gives the church the responsibility and privilege of preaching the Word in the power of the Spirit so that God will be known, said Calvin, "as the Father of a family." God feeds the church, Calvin writes, "with spiritual food" and provides it with everything it needs for human salvation.[40]

The irony to which I draw our attention lies in the manner in which many Protestant churches, who identified themselves as "true" churches according to the standards of the Reformation, found themselves either unable to respond to Martin Luther King's questions or answered them in ways that called into question the very soul of their own ecclesial authenticity and integrity. Reformed Churches, for example, in many cities in the southern United States affirmed that the Word of God *was* in that place faithfully proclaimed and the sacraments *were* faithfully administered; thus, they stood as true and good churches. At the very same moment, as King's car drove through their segregated neighborhoods, King might well look at their soaring spires and wonder, in light of the involvement (or lack of involvement) of these churches in the great matters of civil justice in that day and place, "Who worships here? Who is their God?"

Observing the tacit (and sometimes active) participation of many church members in the subjugation of African Americans in a number of Southern communities, one might ask whether the biblical witness (which sees the liberation of the people of Israel as the central focus of the Old Testament and the prophetic call for justice and righteousness) *is* being faithfully preached there? *Is* the passover (the event of liberation that prefigures and breathes through the sacrament of the Lord's Supper) essential to the Communion celebrated there? Are these church members baptized into the Christ in whom there is now neither Jew nor Greek, neither slave nor free, neither male nor female, in whom economics, class, race, and gender are no longer decisive issues of identity?

To be church is to be "called out from among." This is in large measure the meaning of "ecclesia." How is it possible, then, that the white churches King knew clearly participated in the predominant culture of prejudice and segregation? To be church is to be the Body of Christ. How is it possible that "one" spiritual Body was so clearly divided along color lines that Jim Crow was the real text on any given Sunday—whatever the stated Scripture text for the sermon might be—because every text was read through spectacles ground to the specifications of racial segregation and civil inequality?

In part, the key to this conundrum of ironic self-contradiction lies in the popular understanding of what it means to be the church. We understand that many, if not most, Americans inherited a dual founding of the church in this country. On the one hand, the church that began on these shores was frequently Puritan, that is, Calvinistic and separatist. The Puritan origins were supplemented in time, though not uncritically; the self-understanding of the Protestant church in North America was modified by the influence of other Protestant ecclesiological streams (e.g., Scots-Irish Presbyterianism, the variety of national Lutheran churches, Episcopalianism, and the free churches). The Protestant founders, through an arduous first three generations in the New World, developed a view of the church that placed enormous emphasis on three tests of authentic Christian faith: right teaching and belief (the test of orthodoxy), right behavior (the test of orthopraxy), and right experience and feelings (the ortho-affective test). Authentic Christianity was, according to this founding church, characterized by all three; and the true church was made up of members who could bear testimony to their threefold rectitude. Powerful messages of voluntarism and individualism moved through these churches, messages which assumed that persons by their will united with authentic churches, often in an act of direct rebellion against other churches that were held to be inauthentic.

By the time the third generation of the founders reached advanced years, however, another related but contrasting understanding of the church became prominent in the American colonies. John Locke, a child of English Calvinist parents, and those influenced by Locke, exemplified this understanding. Locke defined the church as follows: "A church, then, I take to be a voluntary society of men, joining themselves together of their own accord in order to the public worshiping of God in such manner as they judge acceptable to Him, and effectual to the salvation of their souls."[41] In place of the tests of authentic Christian faith, Locke emphasized the voluntary banding together of like-minded individuals who sought to promote their own essentially private relationships with God in their assemblies. Churches that identified themselves as "genteel" particularly took a liking to an understanding of the church similar to Locke's. The church became for them virtually a "holy club" or "society" to serve the needs and interests of like-minded private citizens.

This description of church stands in profound contrast to the biblical descriptions of the church. The New Testament does not describe a church as a voluntary society. It certainly does not assume the kind of "like-mindedness" necessary for the banding together of a voluntary society. Instead, in the New Testament, one finds very contrary people summoned together by the Word who overrides, but ultimately does not minimize, their differences. Indeed, the New Testament glories in the plurality and diversity of gifts and perspectives that the Spirit gives to the various "members" of the "Body." As recounted in the New Testament, the first great crisis this early church confronted led to the notion that gentiles could become Christians without embracing the ethnic religious culture of the Jewish followers of Jesus. The unity of this early church, as it was understood by its members, did not rest in the agreement and similarities among themselves but in the Spirit of Christ who made of them one body in which a diversity of giftedness and otherness represents God's presence and activity. The very public nature of God's call to discipleship in the New Testament countered the private nature of religion assumed by many, including Locke (who saw the goal of the church's life as "effectual . . . salvation of their souls"). The primitive communities of faith that sprang into existence in response to the Word of God placed followers of the Way in the public peril of their lives. For the church, the message of the death and Resurrection of Christ became a public and political statement because it was a matter of faith.

In a fascinating twist to the historical development of congregations in the New World, "Lockean" ecclesiology (though recognizing that Locke did not originate this view) combined with the "Puritan." Congregants frequently came to see Protestant churches as voluntary societies, made up of individuals, bodies who based their sense of belonging on similar convictions, beliefs, behaviors, and experiences. This meant that economics, class, race, and gender played key roles in the self-selection of members to particular congregations, within which the faith that was pursued was understood primarily as a private matter. The question of belonging came into play with particular potency among southern Protestant churches, as segregation reigned in pulpits and fellowship halls as surely as it ruled in courthouses and at soda fountains. Discriminatory and racist public policy thus trumped private devotion in the land of religious societies. So the young African-American clergyman driving by the tall steeple marking a white congregation of influence and power in its culture was compelled to ask, "Who worships here? Who is their God?"

One might legitimately fear, in light of this eccesiological turn of plot, that Feuerbach is proven correct in the extreme, that human beings really do worship only the infinite projection of themselves. Perhaps one sees here the ecclesiological echo of colonial theologian Jonathan Edwards's doctrine of God, in which one attributes to God certain qualities such as love and justice. Edwards assumed that all his readers know what love and justice are and that, in order to attribute these qualities to divine being, we merely need to remove imperfections (which it is assumed we will be able to recognize), multiply the pure qualities by the power of infinity, and arrive at the attributes of God.[42] The danger of attempting to do anything *but* a genitive theology confronts us here. We have seen what happens when we universalize the provincial, imagining that we construct Timeless-Universal-Theology when in fact we merely do theology from our own peculiar time and place and claim for it a position of privilege over the theologies of others. But one may also suspect that (to convert Thomas "Tip" O'Neill's oft-quoted political observation) "all theology is local." The very particularity of our theological reflections contains the possibility of apprehending truthfulness and faith in situ. Catholicity is grounded in particularity, and if one abandons the immediate one will miss the eternal altogether. By confessing first our provincial perspectives, we are free to hear the provincial witnesses of one another, and our contradictions can save us from idolatrous claims on behalf of the truth to which we lay claim.

The church we know in our particular context *is* the church, in other words, but it is neither the only church nor the whole church. Churches stand in need of prophetic critique and pastoral comfort from other churches who in their concrete otherness call us to task and bless us. Herein lies the reality of catholicity that transcends our anemic notions of denominational connectionalism and returns us to the full vigor of catholic accountability. Even among Protestant churches, we witness the "Irenaean triad of ecclesial self-definition: the canon of Scripture, the rule of faith, and the teaching authority of bishops" (recognizing the episcopal authority of the office of gathered presbyters).[43] With the understanding that we need one another in order to know who we are, we must have the correction of brothers and sisters whose understanding is valuable to us chiefly because it differs from our own. God does not constitute us as persons in isolation, nor does God leave us to our own ecclesiastical desires and devices. Realizing this, the dogmatic concerns of catholicity must be radically reconceived to take into account the evangelical functionality of catholicity as expressed in particularity, in the discipline of the church catholic over provincial and local misperceptions of Christian faith (as one sees in the witness of the Confessional churches against the "German Christians" in the 1930s and the resulting development of the Barmen Declaration, or among the Christians representing contrasting witnesses within "Reformed" Christendom in the development of the Belhar Declaration in South Africa).

In the concrete reality of churches, we meet an extraordinary variety of traditions, sacred texts, authorities, and hermeneutical filters and lenses through which the Christian faith ("the Christian thing," to borrow the phrase David Kelsey borrows from G. K. Chesterton)[44] in its various manifestations is read and heard and understood, in the midst of the attitudes, interests, loyalties, and attachments that make up our life together.[45] To answer fundamental questions as to the identity of the church (such as King's) we must enter into the varied and sometimes contradictory mix of particular communities of faith. We must hear the questions from within particular contexts and listen to them as questions articulated through Jesus Christ, the Word of God and the human Logos, by the power of the Holy Spirit (honoring the Christ who is present in the community, as Bonhoeffer once said). We must attempt to participate in Christ's answer to these questions by the power of this Spirit, thus entering into catholic and evangelical conversation with the variety of traditions, sacred texts, and other communal authorities, hoping that through such conversation we can come to greater clarity concerning who we are as church and who our God is.

CONFESSIONAL HERMENEUTICS

Our task, then, is to participate in the hearing, reading, and interpretation of holy Scripture in the context of particular communities (in the rich and frequently contradictory ecclesial cocktail of traditions, confessions, and experiences, legends, sagas, and myths that guide and inform the life of this particular community within its larger social, cultural, and historical context) and the reading and interpretation of our particular communities of faith in the context of holy Scripture (in the rich and frequently contradictory mix of traditions, confessions, and experiences, legends, sagas, and myths that make up and surround the canon of Christian Scripture). We simultaneously undertake this exegetical task of reading two sacred and living texts, Bible and people of God, and this makes up our hermeneutical ministry of discernment, which remains fundamental to and necessary for every other ministry task, from administration to preaching to pastoral counseling. Because the two exegetical tasks are necessary and, indeed, mandatory, like John Calvin's conception of wisdom consisting of knowledge of God and knowledge of ourselves, they so intertwine with one another that one cannot discern which precedes the other. Therefore we can discuss them and engage in them in whatever order we wish, realizing that often when we speak of the one task we speak also and simultaneously of the other.

When we approach any particular biblical text, for instance, we do so with the awareness (1) that reading the text represents the problem of being human in and through particular social contexts and thus requires us to be capable of seeing and hearing certain things and being unable to see and hear other things; and (2) that within one's own particular communities of faith, the Trinity is the name of the problem of biblical hermeneutics. The God who, by the power of the Spirit, worked in and through persons in other communities of faith to produce the Scriptures that speak as Word of God is the same God who, by the power of the Spirit, works in and through persons in contemporary communities of faith to hear and receive these Scriptures as Word of God.

When one attempts to discern who we are as a people of God, one is compelled also to ask, What is our relationship to the God through whose Spirit and Word the Scriptures originated and by whose Spirit the Scriptures become God's Word to us? We must attempt this ministry of discernment, of reflective practice and critical judgement, through (and not simply despite) the social and cultural peculiarities of a particular context, realizing that the Scriptures were not produced in spite of the social and cultural peculiarities of their authors and editors but because of and through these very peculiarities. God does not reveal Godself despite the incarnation, in other words, but through the incarnation, because this is who God is. God's revelatory engagement through history is the essential reality of and content of the gospel. There is no transhistorical kernel within God's revelatory engagement through history. God's revelatory engagement with humanity through history is the thing itself in all its husk-i-ness that is God's self-disclosure.

Correspondingly, a "community of faith" or "the church" can never be merely a theoretical construct that in Christian hermeneutics functions as a cipher holding place value in a mathematical equation. Rather, communities of faith are alive in their particularity, alive in their nature as actual human "bodies" of persons living their own sense of history and place, alive in creaturely ambiguity and in the creative and redemptive purposes of the God to whom history is the site of salvation. If we believe we can honor and know the church apart from or beyond the particularity of the church's humanity in historical and social contexts, then we are utterly mistaken. To attempt to construct a theology of "The Church" that is not fundamentally informed by (and shaped by) churches in particularity is to construct a Platonic fiction.

To describe church in a manner that remains faithful to our ethical and hermeneutical tasks, therefore, one must become a kind of participant-observer, skilled in what might be called theological ethnography.[46] But we become precisely that, a *kind* of participant-observer, when our prior relationship to Word and Sacrament defines our vocation and we perform our vocation's hermeneutical and ethical tasks of description in that light. In doing this, two benefits accrue: (1) We are enabled to enter into the living textuality of Christian Scriptures as they are heard and received in the living textuality of particular Christian communities in their vitally and frequently contradictory and countervailing expressions of faith; and (2) we are empowered to enter with new appreciation and understanding into the living contextuality of the confessions, creeds, traditions, legends, sagas, and myths that function authoritatively within our Christian communities, as we discern more clearly both how these expressions arose out of day-to-day life—the conflicts and crises in various communities—and how they have been put to use and have shaped the hearing of Christian Scriptures in distinctive ways.[47]

Perhaps what this approach to describing the church says above all else is that if we hope to answer questions such as "Who worships here? Who is their God?" then we must pay attention to the details of the way our worship functions. We must take seriously every aspect of the articulation of our communal faith *as theological speech*—from the language of the church's architecture to the language of its hymnody, from the conversations congregants enter into in official meetings of their governing boards to the conversations that occur around the coffee pots on Sunday mornings, from the way these Christians shape the stories of faith they recount to their young to the biblical texts that form their corporate self-understanding, that are used to make sense of their piety and personal devotion, and that are used to justify their ethical activities and inactivities in the public realm. But this is only one way of describing church. However richly it rewards our efforts, it stands in need of complement and correction. In the end, the answers to King's questions are deferred in an eschatological move that is as troubling as it is Christianly inevitable. Sunday after Sunday, we bear witness to this reality as we gather round a common table and share a common loaf and a common cup, remembering Christ's death and proclaiming Christ's Resurrection in anticipation that Christ will come again.

Epilogue

ONE OF THE prepublication reviewers of this book wrote that I have not gotten "beyond writing what amounts to a 'preface' to a new ecclesiology" and that I may "want to say that [I] have no idea what the church of the future would or could look like, that it isn't [my] business to know—it is the task of . . . community to invent it." This is precisely my point. I believe God is in the business of inventively and creatively calling forth communities of faith to think and rethink our doctrines of church. However, I also have some concerns on this point.

At an international conference on curriculum that I recently attended, a keynote speaker mapped out what she hoped was a call for a comprehensive, universal, and overarching re-vision of educational programs for children and young adults around the world. She believed she was answering the call of the new millennium to construct a holistic new paradigm. There were elements of her lecture that were, in my view, visionary and not simply trendy cant, but her description of her program possessed the characteristics of an all-controlling meta-vision that could all too easily be made to serve an autocratically enforced and totalitarian philosophical state. She wistfully imagined a conflict-free world united by a single new story, a new human narrative of meaning shared by all persons everywhere. Frankly, she frightened me. I could almost hear the lock-step march of storm troopers in the emotional cadences of her address. While she abstractly espoused certain liberal and humanitarian values many of us would share, her vision was threatening in the extreme to the particular and diverse communities that we inhabit.

I would ask us to consider the value of an alternative. The countervailing particularity of communities of faith, the conflicted state of our value systems within and among these communities, and their diverse narratives of meaning and structures of symbols represent the richness and fullness of churchly life and faith. Rather than yearning for a social group (the word "community" cannot be used here) in which everyone thinks and says the same thing, we would do much better to embrace the pluralistic reality of our diverse communities that give birth to varieties of human life and experiences, viewpoints and visions, that make it possible for us to value very differently very different things. Isaiah Berlin was correct in identifying the desire for absolute axiological monism and for a conflictless society where all values are identical as the very desire that underpins all forms of totalitarianism.[1]

If we are facing the possibility of new ecclesiologies, as I believe we are, then these ecclesiologies must remain doggedly true to their historical rootedness, the canons of sacred texts and confessions, of narratives and communally reinforced habits and practices that provide them with meaning and arise out of the particular forms of life observed in particular communities. Such particularity gives rise to the extraordinary diversity that is the theological reality that we can either face—or deny. I would hope that the reader would find what I have said very suspect if it appears that I am issuing a call for a new ecclesiology that will set at right all others, that will claim for itself a position of privilege above other theological perspectives. On the contrary, as the church faces death in every age and in every place we are presented with many very different (even contradictory) opportunities and ways to trust the God who has died and is risen.

One other reflection in closing: Post-modern theology frequently is marked by a rejection of every conceivable claim to the truth that can authoritatively moderate between claims to truthfulness. This need not be a matter of theological dread. Mark C. Taylor writes: "Postmodernism opens with the sense of irrevocable loss and incurable fault. This wound is inflicted by the overwhelming awareness of death—a death that 'begins with the death of God' and 'ends' with the death of ourselves."[2]

The death of God, however, proved to be not the demise of the divine but merely the destruction of certain confessional and dogmatic cages in which we foolishly believed God to have been successfully imprisoned. Far from dying, God emerged from death unscathed while many all-too-sure-of-themselves systems of theological discourse perished. At the end of the day, the death-of-God movement of a generation ago was turned to serve as an iconoclastic movement on behalf of the worship and the theological endeavors of the church.

The possibility of varieties of understanding has always threatened the watertight theological system. But it is just conceivable that such systems do not serve the church well and that post-modern thought, here, plays its most crucial role in relation to the church precisely in renouncing certainty. Taylor writes, evoking in the process William Blake, "When it no longer seems necessary to reduce manyness to oneness and to translate the equivocal as univocal, it becomes possible to give up the struggle for mastery and to take 'eternal delight' in 'The enigmatical / Beauty of each beautiful enigma.'"[3] Perhaps the best theology can do is to err. Perhaps that is the best any theology can do (and has ever done) in a fallen world. But perhaps it is by making these errors that we honor the God who stands free and unfettered beyond the grasp of every statement.

If the best we can do is make particular theological mistakes—on the basis of the faith claims made in particular communities of faith, in conversation with other communities of faith, and in reflection on sacred texts that have emerged from past communities of faith—and, if there is no foundation on which we can build our faith claims other than the foundation who is Jesus Christ, whose very life is a renunciation of every name we try to attach to God in our vain attempts to control God, then I want to say that the routes I have traversed in this book are the mistakes I want to make on the basis of the faith I have been given in the communities of faith embedded in the human cultures in which I live.

This is theological play; but this is theological play with a serious intent and with an end beyond itself. This is theological play in an ambiguous world under the unambiguous claim of the kingdom of God. I believe this is true. But in the face of the living God and in the midst of the church facing death I am prepared to stand corrected.

Notes

Introduction

1. Claude Lévi-Strauss, *Tristes Tropiques: An Anthropological Study of Primitive Societies in Brazil,* tr. John Russell (New York: Atheneum, 1969), 100.

2. See Roland Barthes, *Criticism and Truth,* tr. Katrine Pilcher Keuneman (Minneapolis: University of Minnesota Press, 1987; first published in France, 1966), 75–76.

3. Charles Gordon Browne and James Edward Swallow, editorial note to "Oration II: In Defence of His Flight to Pontus, and His Return, After His Ordination to the Priesthood, with an Exposition of the Character of the Priestly Office," *Nicene and Post-Nicene Fathers of the Christian Church,* second series, ed. Philip Schaff and Henry Wace (Grand Rapids: Eerdmans, 1983), 7: 204.

4. See Anthony Meredith, *The Cappadocians* (Crestwood, N.Y.: St. Vladimir's Seminary Press, 1995), 39–42.

5. Gregory, "Oration II," in Schaff and Wace, *Nicene and Post-Nicene Fathers,* 7: 214.

One. The Church Faces Death

1. "Disappearing Church," *Christian Century,* March 18–25, 1992, 297.

2. Ian Bradley, *Marching to the Promised Land: Has the Church a Future?* (London: John Murray, 1992). As of 1995, the figure of annual membership loss was reported in the neighborhood of seventeen thousand. *Life and Work,* May 1995, 5. The most recent statistics from the Kirk's Department of Ministry (courtesy of Heather Delaney) show a total membership at the end of 1996 of 680,062, which represents a decline from its reported membership for 1994 of 715,571. The number of churches declined over the same period from 1,619 to 1,603.

3. Robin Hill, "Strolling to the Precipice," *Life and Work,* January 1996, 3. The issue of age, and the necessity of addressing a viable witness to the young, surfaces again in an article by Julie Smith, "Get Relevant," *Life and Work,* March 1996, 25.

4. Bill Longmuir, "Forward Planning Pays Off," *Life and Work,* September 1995, 14; Robin Hill, "Another Slice, Minister?" and a brief piece on clergy stipends by George Hamilton, both in *Life and Work,* May 1995, 4, 5. The reports to the General Assembly of 1995 were particularly preoccupied with these concerns, as one sees in the "preview of reports being considered by commissioners in Edinburgh" (May 20 –26) in the May issue of *Life and Work,* 19.

5. An especially interesting article in this regard is John Ferguson, "Courting Teamwork," *Life and Work,* February 1996, 20, which asks the question, "Can presbyteries be relevant to today's Church?" And a brief editorial comment in the same journal asks: "If the General As-

sembly of the Church of Scotland is so important, why don't more people take it more seriously?" The editor continues: "Any neutral outsider visiting 121 George Street [the national headquarters of the Church of Scotland, in Edinburgh] at this time of year might well come away with the idea that assembly week ranks alongside Easter and Christmas as a major festival of the Presbyterian Church. But if our visitor were to ask around congregations, would he or she find the same enthusiasm in parishes and pews? I have my doubts, not least because it's often hard to see how the Christian faith is strengthened and promoted by many of the deliberations and deliverances which roll out of the Assembly Hall year by year. It's clear that a great many people couldn't care less about the assembly and its workings—possibly because they view it as an annual celebration of Church administration, which for six days in May argues much, yet creates little of lasting significance. If this view is mistaken, then it must be up to the General Assembly to prove them, and me, wrong." *Life and Work,* May 1996, editor's comments on contents page.

6. Note Iain Torrance, "Between Legalism and Liberalism: Wisdom in Christian Ethics," in *But Where Shall Wisdom Be Found,* ed. Alan Main (Aberdeen: Aberdeen University Press, 1995), 64–71. Note also Ivor Gibson, "Recovering Belief," *Life and Work,* January 1996, 21–22. And, relative to issues of ministry and Gaelic culture, see Donald E. Meeks, *The Scottish Highlands: The Churches and Gaelic Culture* (Geneva: World Council of Churches Publications, 1996).

7. Iain Paton, "A Sign of Vitality," *Life and Work,* September 1994, 15. William Storrar strikes a similar chord in his quincentenary lecture at the University of Aberdeen, "The Decline of the Kirk," published in the university's *Divinity Alumni Association Newsletter,* Autumn 1997, no. 18, 5–8.

8. Office of the General Assembly, Presbyterian Church (U.S.A.), *Minutes, 208th General Assembly,* Jan. 1–Dec. 31, 1996, part 2. I appreciate the efforts of Kris Valerius, assistant to the manager for statistical reports at the Office of the General Assembly, for her confirmation of these statistics.

9. Statistics were reported in the "Daily Summary," June 29, 1996 by Jerry Van Marter.

10. Coalter, Milton J., John M. Mulder, and Louis B. Weeks, eds., *The Presbyterian Predicament: Six Perspectives* (1990); *The Confessional Mosaic: Presbyterians and Twentieth-Century Theology* (1990); *The Mainstream Protestant "Decline": The Presbyterian Pattern* (1990); *The Diversity of Discipleship: Presbyterians and Twentieth-Century Christian Witness* (1991); *The Pluralistic Vision: Presbyterians and Mainstream Protestant Education and Leadership* (1992); *The Organizational Revolution: Presbyterians and American Denominationalism* (1992). These seven volumes, all published by Westminster/John Knox Press, Louisville, were summarized in *The Re-Forming Tradition: Presbyterians and Mainstream Protestantism* (1992).

11. Coalter, Mulder, and Weeks, *The Mainstream Protestant "Decline,"* 19.

12. Kenneth L. Woodward, "Dead End for the Mainline?" *Newsweek,* August 9, 1993, 46–48.

13. Darrell L. Guder's essay, "Locating a Reformed Theology of Evangelism in a Pluralistic World," in *How Shall We Witness? Faithful Evangelism in a Reformed Tradition,* ed. Milton J. Coalter and Virgil Cruz (Louisville: Westminster/John Knox Press, 1995), 165–86, (editorial introduction, xix–xx). Milton J. Coalter says (commenting on Guder's essay in the introduction) the church "finds its direction from the invigorating discovery of good news for private and public human life found uniquely in Jesus Christ. In Christ the church finds embodied the *missio Dei* (the mission of God) to create *koinonia* (community) through both *kerygma* (the good news of salvation proclaimed) and *diakonia* (the good news of salvation enacted through service)."

14. *Christian Century,* August 12–19, 1992, 740.

15. "Problems Plague UMC's Study of Problems," *Christian Century,* February 2–9, 1994, 97.

16. "United Methodists Show Age, Says Survey," *Christian Century,* July 5–12, 1995, 673.

17. "Methodism Slated to Disappear in Britain?" *Christian Century,* May 8, 1996, 507.

18. Woodward, "Dead End," 47.

19. Loren Mead, *The Once and Future Church: Reinventing the Congregation for a New Mission Frontier* (Washington, D.C.: Alban Institute, 1991), v.

20. For instance, Sang Eui Chun, "A Praxis Credo: A Practical Evangelism Model from a Comparative Study of the Korean Methodist Church and the United Methodist Church," Saint Paul School of Theology, Kansas City, Missouri, dissertation, 1994.

21. Note, for example, Douglas John Hall, *The Future of the Church: Where Are We Headed?* (United Church of Canada: United Church of Canada Publishing House, 1989) and "An Awkward Church," Theology and Worship Occasional Paper no. 5 (Louisville: Presbyterian Church, U.S.A.); Mead, *Once and Future Church*; Peter Hodgson, *Revisioning the Church: Ecclesial Freedom in the New Paradigm* (Minneapolis: Fortress Press, 1988); Thomas E. Frank, "Ecclesial Vision and the Realities of Congregational Life," *Quarterly Review,* Spring 1992, 3–17; Leander E. Keck, *The Church Confident* (Nashville: Abingdon Press, 1993), the cover of which is embellished with the quote from Charles Clayton Morrison's Lyman Beecher Lectures of 1939, "Christianity can repent, but it must not whimper"; and J. Edward Carothers, *The Paralysis of Mainstream Protestant Leadership* (Nashville: Abingdon Press, 1990).

22. Floyd L. Berrier, "A New Context for Doing United Methodist Theology," Columbia Theological Seminary, Decatur, Georgia, dissertation, 1990.

23. See Marsha G. Witten, *All Is Forgiven: The Secular Message in American Protestantism* (Princeton: Princeton University Press, 1993), and, from a different perspective, Donald E. Miller, *Reinventing American Protestantism: Christianity in the New Millennium* (Berkeley: University of California Press, 1997).

24. As quoted in Jacques Derrida, *The Gift of Death,* tr. David Wills (Chicago: University of Chicago Press, 1995), 16.

25. Derrida, *Gift of Death,* 82.

26. For an illuminating analysis of the theological dimensions of Derrida's work, see John D. Caputo, *The Prayers and Tears of Jacques Derrida: Religion without Religion* (Bloomington: Indiana University Press, 1997), in which the apophatic and the messianic (or prophetic/ethical) aspects of Derrida's thought are perceptively analyzed. Walter Lowe also discerns the moral force of Derrida's thought in his excellent study *Theology and Difference: The Wound of Reason* (Bloomington: Indiana University Press, 1993), 55–74, 127–45.

27. Derrida, *Gift of Death,* 41.

28. Thus Paul Ricoeur can say that "the price we have to pay to follow Jesus is not unrelated to the question of his identity. Peter seeks a glorious Christ and cannot accept the fact that Christ is the Suffering Servant, must be the Suffering Servant, sung of by Second Isaiah." Ricoeur critiques the attempt to use God as a means of security; he writes, "It is just this attempt to make use of God as a guarantee for our desire to have a guarantee that seems to me most called into question by the expression 'letting go of self.' Faith, Eberhard Jüngel, a theologian at Tübingen, has said is the overthrowing of the guarantee, it is the risk of a life placed under the sign of the suffering Christ. Our passage adds to this 'letting go of self,' 'taking up one's cross.' This powerful expression brings us back to the context deliberately chosen by the Synoptic authors for the verses we are considering, namely, the announcement by Jesus of his imminent passion. What bond is there between the invitation addressed to Christians to take

up their cross and Jesus' announcement of the necessity of the passion?" From a sermon Ricoeur preached on the text Matthew 16:25, "Whoever Loses Their Life for My Sake Will Find It," in the Rockefeller Chapel at the University of Chicago, November 25, 1984, in *Figuring the Sacred: Religion, Narrative and Imagination*, tr. David Pellauer, ed. Mark I. Wallace (Minneapolis: Fortress Press, 1995), 284, 288.

29. Derrida, *Gift of Death*, 16.

30. *Ibid.*, 41.

31. Martin Heidegger, *Being and Time*, tr. John Macquarrie and Edward Robinson (Oxford: Basil Blackwell, 1962), 314.

32. H. Richard Niebuhr wrote: "Again Jesus Christ is the symbolic form with which the self understands itself, with the aid of which it guides and forms itself in its actions and its sufferings. Paul's statement, 'It is no longer I that live but Christ who lives within me,' runs to the extreme of identification. Less extreme are all the symbolic statements of those Christians who think of and, in part, conduct their lives as imitations of Christ, as conformities to his mind; who follow him, are his disciples, live, suffer, and die with him." *The Responsible Self: An Essay in Christian Moral Philosophy* (New York: Harper and Row, 1963), 156.

33. Kathleen Norris understands the theological etymology of "martyr": "[A] martyr is not a model to be imitated, but a witness, one who testifies to a new reality." Norris, *The Cloister Walk* (New York: Riverhead Books, 1996), 191.

34. Dietrich Bonhoeffer, *The Cost of Discipleship*, rev. ed. (New York: Macmillan, 1963), 98.

35. The "self-justification" or "justification 'by the law'" that Pauline literature frequently casts as the antithesis to the gospel of Christ. Marcus Barth, *Ephesians 1–3*, Anchor Bible Commentary (Garden City, N.Y.: Doubleday, 1979), 244–48.

36. Derrida, *Gift of Death*, 43–44.

37. *Ibid.*, 44.

38. *Ibid.*, 45.

39. *Ibid.*, 44.

40. I am particularly indebted, at this point, to my colleague Cynthia Rigby, "Free To Be Human: Limits, Possibilities, and the Sovereignty of God," *Theology Today* 53 (April 1996), no. 1, and to Colin E. Gunton, *The One, the Three and the Many: God, Creation and the Culture of Modernity: The 1992 Bampton Lectures* (Cambridge: Cambridge University Press, 1993), 210–231.

41. Emmanuel Levinas, "Time and the Other," in *The Levinas Reader*, ed. Seán Hand (Oxford: Blackwell, 1989), 43. "*Eros*, strong as death" is a reference to Song of Solomon 8:6. See also Paul Ricoeur, *Oneself as Another*, tr. Kathleen Blamey (Chicago: University of Chicago Press, 1992).

42. Levinas, "Time and the Other," 43. Also E. Levinas, *Basic Philosophical Writings*, ed. Andriaan T. Peperzak, Simon Critchley, and Robert Bernasconi (Bloomington: Indiana University Press, 1996), 1–10. Compare Caputo's illuminating interpretation of Derrida's *"Différance,"* in *Prayers and Tears*, 1–20; and Colin Davis's general introduction, *Levinas* (Notre Dame: University of Notre Dame Press, 1996), 34–62.

43. Levinas, "Time and the Other," 52. Levinas in his observations at this point bears an exceptional resonance with certain aspects of John Macmurray's 1953–1954 Gifford Lectures delivered under the title "The Form of the Personal," especially the second book, *Persons In Relation*, in which Macmurray writes: "In talking of the Self as agent we accepted the traditional abstraction from existence, and initiated a discussion of the *concept* of action. Now we have to take the practical standpoint for granted, and consider the Agent, not as an abstract

concept, but in its concrete actuality as existent. The appropriate term here is the term 'person'. Any 'self'—that is to say, any agent—is an existing being, a person. At this point, therefore, our discussion enters the field of the personal. The theme of the present volume can be stated simply. The idea of an isolated agent is self-contradictory. Any agent is necessarily in relation to the Other. Apart from this essential relation he does not exist. But, further, the Other in this constitutive relation must itself be personal. Persons, therefore, are constituted by their mutual relation to one another. 'I' exist only as one element in the complex 'You and I'. We have to discover how this ultimate fact can be adequately thought, that is to say, symbolized in reflection." John Macmurray, *Persons in Relation* (London: Faber and Faber, 1961; new ed. 1991), 24 (new ed.), and, in this immediate context, see also Macmurray's discussion titled "Mother and Child" (44–63).

44. Compare Colin Gunton's extraordinary analysis of trinitarian theology *The One, The Three and The Many*, 41–73, 129–79; and his earlier study *The Promise of Trinitarian Theology* (Edinburgh: T. and T. Clark, 1991), especially 86–103.

45. Krister Stendahl, *Final Account: Paul's Letter to the Romans* (Minneapolis: Fortress Press, 1995) 27.

46. Derrida, *Gift of Death*, 46.

47. *Ibid.*, 50–51.

48. Pheme Perkins, "The Gospel of Mark," in *The New Interpreter's Bible Commentary*, (Nashville: Abingdon Press, 1995) 8: 626.

49. Levinas, "Time and the Other," 41.

50. *Ibid.*, 41. Levinas continues later: "What can we infer from this analysis of death? Death becomes the limit of the subject's virility, the virility made possible by the hypostasis of the heart of anonymous being, and manifest in the phenomenon of the present, in the light. . . . What is important about the approach of death is that at a certain moment we are no longer able to be able [nous ne 'pouvons plus pouvoir']. It is exactly thus that the subject loses its very mastery as a subject" (42).

51. William Stringfellow, *Instead of Death* (New York: Seabury Press, rev. ed., 1976), 9. Stringfellow speaks, in another context, of the power of the fear of death that becomes a dread of living: "The transcendence of the power and presence of death in just such dimensions of dread as these is what the death in Christ . . . concerns. The secret of the relationship of Anthony [Towne] and myself was not that we were able to identify and affirm each other in defiance of dread, but that we were each enabled to apprehend and mediate to the other the truth that the Word of God alone has the ability to identify and affirm either of us as persons or to offer the same to any other human being. The peril in the experience of dread is in succumbing to the idolatry of death in one's own being. The extent to which this society is death-ridden and the culture motivated by the worship of death . . . constitutes relentless pressure on everyone to surrender and to conform to that idolatry." Stringfellow, *A Simplicity of Faith: My Experience in Mourning* (Nashville: Abingdon Press, 1982), 49–50. See also *A Keeper of the Word: Selected Writings of William Stringfellow*, ed. Bill Wylie Kellermann (Grand Rapids: Eerdmans, 1994); and Charles L. Campbell's perceptive article, "Principalities, Powers and Preaching: Learning from William Stringfellow," *Interpretation* 51 (October 1997), no. 4, 384–401.

52. Gregory Bateson's comments on power's tendency to corrupt are apt in this context. Bateson maintains, against Lord Acton's popular axiom ("Power tends to corrupt and absolute power corrupts absolutely"), that "[w]hat is true is that the *idea* of power corrupts." In fact, it is the *idea* of the power of death (disclosed in the apprehension of death) that is most

devastating to the life of the church. Death's threat is, in the face of resurrection, a hollow one. Death's power *is* apprehension. Gregory Bateson, *Steps to an Ecology of Mind* (Northvale, N.J.: Jacob Aronson, 1972; new ed., 1987), 494. Bateson's remarks appeared originally in a paper he gave entitled "Pathologies of Epistemology," at the Second Conference on Mental Health in Asia and the Pacific, 1969, at the East-West Center, Hawaii. Lord Acton's oft-quoted words appeared in a letter to Bishop Mandell Creighton, April 3, 1887. Michael Jinkins and Deborah Bradshaw Jinkins, *Power and Change in Parish Ministry* (Washington, D.C.: Alban Institute, 1991), 82.

53. G. K. Chesterton, *The Everlasting Man* (London: Hodder and Stoughton, 1925), 288.

54. *Ibid.,* 290.

55. This, to some degree, speaks to the present preoccupation of many in the Church of Scotland with a return to the Westminster standards or, even, to the symbols of Dort, and in the Presbyterian Church (U.S.A.) variously with the so-called essential tenets or fundamentals of the Reformed faith. These churches, apprehensive at the prospect of institutional death, alternately reach for a return to a seemingly unequivocal set of credal standards that provide identity, and for the establishment of identity in the flux of constant change (thus the frequent appropriation—and misappropriation—of the phrase "Ecclesia reformata, semper reformanda"). Yet the church as church has only one identity that *teleologically* enshrouds its entire existence from birth to death, its naming in and through the baptismal waters of which it is reminded at its communication of the Eucharist. See George W. Stroup, "A Lover's Quarrel: Theology and the Church," in *The Seminary: A School of the Church: Speeches from the Presidential Inauguration* (Austin: Austin Presbyterian Theological Seminary, November 14, 1997).

56. Derrida, *Gift of Death,* 51.

57. Eduard Schweizer, *Lordship and Discipleship* (London: SCM Press, 1960), 16.

58. The persistent distrust of the church held by various national political interests is grounded in the awareness that the church's sworn allegiance lies elsewhere—with an-Other. Note Arthur M. Schlesinger, Jr., *The Cycles of American History* (Boston: Houghton Mifflin, 1986) and, more recently, Harvey C. Mansfield, *Machiavelli's Virtue* (Chicago: University of Chicago Press, 1996).

59. Reinhold Niebuhr, *Moral Man and Immoral Society* (New York: Scribner's, 1932), 263–64. Only a very superficial reading of Niebuhr could emerge with the view that he abandons the public and corporate realm to the motives of self-interest and self-preservation. In the name of Christ, he argues for a power that would counter injustice. He enters into this realm with eyes open to the devastation that unprincipled power can accomplish, and he calls for a responsibility that counts the cost and pays the price—particularly when that price is a cross.

60. The problem with *conceiving* of church, which is also the problem of *perceiving* church as community of faith—a problem that neither Kierkegaard nor Derrida seem able to solve—arises, at least in part, from our inadequate understanding of community. The conventional understanding of community is primarily that of some sort of public assemblage or static grouping to which we belong sociologically or which we "attend." In fact, each individual is the bearer and beneficiary of a variety of communities that make up that which we term "community"—persons in relationship. There is no single homogeneous group to which a person belongs and can point to as his or her community. Rather the individual lives through community specifically by living in relationship in response to a variety of relationships. Yet what is *there* is the flux of persons in relationship, which, motion picture–like, relates to persons as community. Any person might conceivably pass through a dozen (or more) such "com-

munities" in a week. Peculiarities of language mark the boundaries of these communities. Technical, colloquial, religious, philosophical languages, the native languages of various communities, are carried in the person moving through the communities, as the person speaks in and through the various communities. An individual does not generally speak the language of one community in another community unless some members of the communities overlap and that individual finds a confluence of shared signs and understanding. Again, the person bears the communities in him- or herself. The person is never—so long as she or he speaks— without community (which is to say, without the matrix of relationships that define and give meaning to the person and the person's actions). One might almost say that all communities are virtual; that is, "community" is not simply a single, unequivocal corpus made up of a particular set of persons. Rather, community that exists in the radicality of its particularity is also, and at the same time, an abstract construct. It is not *there* statically. Indeed, one of the most prominent attributes of community—and of all relationships—is the absence of the other. Levinas indicates this when he writes: "The pathos of love, however, consists in an insurmountable duality of beings. It is a relationship with what always slips away" ("Time and Other," 49). And: "The relationship with the Other is the absence of the other; not absence pure and simple, not the absence of pure nothingness, but absence in a horizon of the future, and absence that is time" (51). See also Alan J. Torrance, *Persons in Communion: Trinitarian Description and Human Participation* (Edinburgh: T. and T. Clark, 1996), especially 325–55.

Two. De-scribing Church

1. Václav Havel, "A Word about Words," in *Open Letters: Selected Writings, 1965–1990*, ed. Paul Wilson (New York: Vintage Books, 1992), 383.

2. *Ibid.*, 383. Havel speaks also of the way in which the meanings of words, for instance "socialism" or "capitalism," are subject to a kind of contextual slippage in his essay, "What I Believe," in his *Summer Meditations* (New York: Knopf, 1992), 60–62. In fact, Havel explains that he has quit using the word "capitalism" because of its associations (63). His comments reflect an understanding similar to that of Wittgenstein, who suggested that sometimes a word has to be "withdrawn from language and sent for cleaning—then it can be put back into circulation." Ludwig Wittgenstein, *Culture and Value*, ed. G. H. von Wright and Heikki Nyman, tr. Peter Winch (Chicago: University of Chicago Press, 1980), 39.

3. Havel, "A Word about Words," 381.

4. *Ibid.*, 383–384.

5. *Ibid.*, 378.

6. *Ibid.*, 388.

7. *Ibid.*, 382.

8. Colin Gunton, to whom I have already referred, argues for an understanding of God and creation that values particularity and a "constitutive relatedness"; that "every thing is what it is and not another thing entails the otherness of everything to everything else." This distinction in unity is the hallmark of the divine trinity and of relationality between God and world, and among humanity. Gunton, *The One, The Three and The Many*, 41–73. See also John Macmurray, "The Celebration of Communion," in *Persons in Relation*, 147–65.

9. Fyodor Dostoyevsky, *The Brothers Karamazov*, tr. Constance Garnett, ed. Manuel Komroff (New York: New American Library, 1957) 1.5.5., 234–35.

10. Augustine, *Confessions*, tr. Henry Chadwick (Oxford: Oxford University Press, 1991), I.i.(1), 3.

11. Second Helvetic Confession, chapter XVII.

12. Havel, "A Word about Words," 382.

13. Tertullian, "The Martyrdom of Perpetua and Felicitas," in *The Ante-Nicene Fathers,* ed. Alexander Roberts and James Donaldson (Grand Rapids: Eerdmans, 1980), 3:705.

14. The origins of "describe" (also "descrybe") are Latin through Old French and Middle English ("descrive"). (The misspelling "dis-scribe" arose from misunderstanding, a confusion of this word with those words taking the prefix "des-" or "dis-". The Latin *describere* means simply "to write (*scribe*) down (*de*)." Modern usages, like Jeremy Taylor's (1649), carry this meaning: "Christ our Lawgiver hath described all his Father's will in Sanctions and Signatures of laws." The ordinary contemporary sense of the word, which logically derives from the root meaning, is stated as follows: "To set forth in words, written or spoken, by reference to qualities, recognizable features, or characteristic marks; to give a detailed or graphic account of" (James Murray et al., *Oxford English Dictionary*). As Joseph Shipley notes, there is also a close linguistic connection between the Latin root *scribere* and the medieval *shrines* or coffers or arks in which writing materials and manuscripts—rare, precious and expensive—were kept, and the reliquaries, shrines, coffers, or arks in which were kept the relics of martyrs. Joseph T. Shipley, *Dictionary of Word Origins* (New York: Philosophical Library, 1945), 322.

15. Havel, "A Word about Words," 383–84.

16. *Ibid.,* 384.

17. This line of reflection was recommended by my colleague Stanley Robertson Hall, associate professor of liturgics at Austin Seminary.

18. Gerhard Kittel, *Theological Dictionary of the New Testament,* ed. and tr. Geoffrey W. Bromiley (Grand Rapids: Eerdmans, 1964), 2: 169.

19. *Ibid.,* 170.

20. Note Fred Craddock's discussion in *Preaching* (Nashville: Abingdon Press, 1985), 55–60.

21. The epigraph's source is Claus Westermann, *What Does the Old Testament Say about God?* Sprunt Lectures for 1977, Union Seminary in Virginia, Richmond, Virginia (Atlanta: John Knox Press, 1979), 41–42.

22. Carlyle Marney, *Priests to Each Other* (Valley Forge: Judson Press, 1974), 73.

23. *Ibid.,* 74.

24. Karl Barth, *Learning Jesus Christ through the Heidelberg Catechism,* tr. Shirley C. Guthrie, Jr. (Grand Rapids: Eerdmans, 1964), 111–12.

25. Eberhard Busch, *Karl Barth: His Life from Letters and Autobiographical Texts,* tr. John Bowden (Philadelphia: Fortress Press, 1975), 224.

26. As when Stephen W. Hawking says, "An expanding universe does not preclude a creator, but it does place limits on when he might have carried out his job!" *A Brief History of Time: From the Big Bang to Black Holes* (London: Bantam, 1988), 9. Friedrich Schleiermacher, *The Christian Faith,* ed. H. R. Mackintosh, tr. J. S. Stewart (Edinburgh: T. and T. Clark, 1928), 16–18.

27. Gunton, *The One, The Three and The Many,* 55. Also see Colin E. Gunton, *The Triune Creator: A Historical and Systematic Study* (Grand Rapids: Eerdmans, 1998), 146–74.

28. Eberhard Jüngel, *God as the Mystery of the World: On the Foundation of Theology of the Crucified One in the Dispute between Theism and Atheism,* tr. Darrell L. Guder (Grand Rapids: Eerdmans, 1983), 3–42, especially section 3, "The Basic Theological Uncertainty (Aporia) of Christian Talk about God."

29. Karl Barth, *Church Dogmatics* ed. G. W. Bromiley and T. F. Torrance, tr. T. H. L. Parker

et al. (Edinburgh: T. and T. Clark, 1957), II. 1. 61. "We might say of this revelation of His name that it consists in the refusal of a name, but even in the form of this substantial refusal, it is still really revelation, communication and illumination. . . . God is the One whose being can be investigated only in the form of a continuous question as to His action." Also Charles Wood, *The Formation of Christian Understanding: Theological Hermeneutics,* 2nd ed. (Valley Forge: Trinity Press International, 1993), 34–35.

30. John of Damascus, *Exposition of the Orthodox Faith,* chapter 16 in Schaff and Wace, *Nicene and Post-Nicene Fathers,* 9: 38. Also Ambrosios Giakalis, *Images of the Divine: The Theology of Icons at the Seventh Ecumenical Council* (Leiden: E. J. Brill, 1994); Jaroslav Pelikan, *Imago Dei: The Byzantine Apologia for Icons* (Princeton: Princeton University Press, 1990); also Paul C. Finney, "Antecedents of Byzantine Iconoclasm: Christian Evidence before Constantine" and Stephen Gero, "Byzantine Iconoclasm and the Failure of a Medieval Reformation," in *The Image and the Word: Confrontations in Judaism, Christianity and Islam,* ed. Joseph Gutmann (Missoula, Mont.: Scholars Press, 1977), 27–62.

31. John of Damascus, *On Divine Images: Three Apologies against Those Who Attack the Divine Images,* tr. David Anderson (Crestwood, N.Y.: St. Vladimir's Seminary Press, 1980), 15–16.

32. The sense of "work" meant here is indicated in John Tavener's introduction to *Ikons: Meditations in Words and Music,* co-authored with Mother Thekla (London: Fount, 1995), where he says: "Let us begin again and again and again, but let us always begin anew as if for the first time, picking up all that we have learnt from both the *via negativa* and the *via positiva.* . . . We believe and yet we know nothing" (ix). And as he speaks of the manner in which he listens to the gospels, then goes to work, to pray, to reflect on the lives and writings of the saints, to talk with and listen to his colleague in faith, Mother Thekla, allowing all of this to be a work of praise to produce musical icons, one gains a sense of the manner in which work is worship and worship work especially in the making of images.

33. T. F. Torrance provides a valuable discussion of this patristic conception of the Word in *The Trinitarian Faith: An Evangelical Theology of the Ancient Catholic Church* (Edinburgh: T. and T. Clark, 1988), 68–75, 117–45.

34. Notice particularly the excellent opening chapter of Rebecca Chopp, *The Power to Speak: Feminism, Language, God* (New York: Crossroad, 1992), 10–39.

35. Umberto Eco, *The Role of the Reader: Explorations in the Semiotics of Texts* (Bloomington: Indiana University Press, 1979), 3–5; also 47–66.

36. John of Damascus, *On Divine Images,* 15.

37. Rebecca Chopp, unpublished response to Walter Brueggemann, Annual Meeting of the American Academy of Religion/ Society for Biblical Literature, Frontiers in Biblical Scholarship: The Endowment for Biblical Lecture Series, Philadelphia, November 19, 1995, 2.

38. *Ibid.,* 4–5.

39. G. K. Chesterton, *Orthodoxy* (London: Bodley Head, 1908), 83.

40. Erich Zenger, *A God of Vengeance? Understanding the Psalms of Divine Wrath,* tr. Linda M. Maloney (Louisville: Westminster/ John Knox Press, 1994), 43–44. The concept of "semantic shock" to which Zenger alludes derives from Harald Weinrich, "Semantik der kühnen Metapher," in *Theorie der Metapher,* ed. A Haverkamp (Darmstadt, 1983). As Zenger notes, "the 'contradictoriness' of the metaphors . . . give them their 'bold character' "(99). The second quote in Zenger's statement is drawn from Jürgen Werbick, *Bilder sind Wege. Eine Gotteslehre* (Munich, 1992). See also Michael Jinkins, *In the House of the Lord: Inhabiting the Psalms of Lament* (Collegeville, Minn.: Liturgical Press, 1998) and Michael Jinkins and Ste-

phen Breck Reid, "God's Godforsakenness: The Cry of Dereliction as an Utterance within the Trinity," *Horizons in Biblical Theology: An International Dialogue* 19 (June 1997), no. 1, 33–57.

41. John of Damascus, *On Divine Images*, 19–31.

42. Stanley Hauerwas, *In Good Company: The Church as Polis* (Notre Dame: University of Notre Dame, 1995), 23–24. This essay was previously published as "What Could It Mean for the Church to Be Christ's Body? A Question without a Clear Answer," *Scottish Journal of Theology* 48 (Winter 1995), no. 1.

43. *Ibid.*, 24.

44. For an attempt to trace out some of the implications of this fact in the praxis of ecclesial and other forms of leadership see Michael Jinkins and Deborah Bradshaw Jinkins, *The Character of Leadership: Political Realism and Public Virtue in Nonprofit Organizations* (San Francisco: Jossey-Bass, 1998).

Three. Taxonomies

1. Not only did Aristotle understand the development of categories of classification as essential to understanding, he provided the methodology of analysis with its hallmark, departmentalization: "The compound should always be resolved into the simple elements or least parts of the whole. We must therefore look at the elements of which the state is composed, in order that we may see in what the different kinds of rule differ from one another, and whether any scientific result can be attained about each one of them." Aristotle, *The Politics*, ed. Stephen Everson, tr. Jonathan Barnes (Cambridge: Cambridge University Press, 1988), I.1. [1].

2. As H. Richard Niebuhr observed, Troeltsch, instructed by his colleague Weber, developed a taxonomy of religious social organization: the church, the sect and mysticism. Ernst Troeltsch, *The Social Teaching of the Christian Churches*, tr. Olive Wyon, ed. H. Richard Niebuhr (New York: Harper, 1960), 1: 10. Max Weber, *The Sociology of Religion*, tr. Ephraim Fischoff (Boston: Beacon Press, 1963).

3. Avery Dulles, *Models of the Church* (New York: Doubleday, 1st ed. 1978; expanded ed. 1987).

4. H. Richard Niebuhr, *Christ and Culture* (New York: Harper and Row, 1951).

5. Mead, *Once and Future Church*.

6. Dulles, *Models of the Church*, 15.

7. *Ibid.*, 16–17.

8. *Ibid.*, 17.

9. *Ibid.*, 17.

10. *Ibid.*, 19. Dulles notes, at this point, Paul Minear's list of ninety-six ecclesiological images in *Images of the Church in the New Testament* (Philadelphia: Westminster Press, 1960).

11. Dulles, *Models of the Church*, 28.

12. *Ibid.*, 32.

13. *Ibid.*, 34.

14. *Ibid.*, 47.

15. *Ibid.*, 204.

16. *Ibid.*, 203.

17. Niebuhr, *Christ and Culture*, 2.

18. *Ibid.*, 4–11.

19. *Ibid.*, 10.

20. *Ibid.*, 39–40.

21. *Ibid.*, 253; certainly his observations in the final chapter (tellingly given the Kierke-gaardian title "A 'Concluding Unscientific Postscript'") demonstrate his appreciation for the contradictory character of life in human community. Though his comments in that context do not bear directly on the argument, they are worth remembering: "Without loyalty and trust in causes and communities, existential selves do not live or exercise freedom or think. Righteous and unrighteous, we live by faith. But our faiths are broken and bizarre; our causes are many and in conflict with each other. In the name of loyalty to one cause we betray an-other; and in our distrust of all, we seek our little unsatisfactory satisfactions and become faithless to our companions." Also note Jacques Derrida, *Writing and Difference*, tr. Alan Bass (Chicago: University of Chicago Press, 1978), 3–63.

22. Niebuhr, *Christ and Culture*, 40–41 and 45–82.

23. *Ibid.*, 72, where Niebuhr comments on the nature of this contradiction: "It is remark-able to what extent the ethics of second-century Christianity—as summarized for instance in *The Teaching of the Twelve* and the *Epistle of Barnabas*—contains material extraneous to the New Testament. These Christians, who thought of themselves as a new 'race' distinct from Jews and Gentiles, borrowed from the laws and customs of those from whom they had sepa-rated what they needed for the common life but had not received from their own authority. The situation is similar in the case of the monastic rules. Benedict of Nursia seeks Scriptural foundation for all his regulations and counsels; but the New Testament does not suffice him, nor does the Bible as a whole; and he must find, in old reflections on human experience in so-cial life, rules by means of which to govern the new community. The spirit in which both Scriptural and non-Scriptural regulations are presented also shows how impossible it is to be only a Christian without reference to culture."

24. *Ibid.*, 41 and 83–115.

25. *Ibid.*, 83.

26. *Ibid.*, 92.

27. *Ibid.*, 99, in which context Niebuhr's comments are directed primarily to the heirs of Ritschl.

28. *Ibid.*, 101–2.

29. *Ibid.*, 102. Sectarian Fundamentalism in the Christian context is largely a product of the Enlightenment, which it scorns. Even its critique of science on the basis of its under-standing of a literalist reading of an inerrant Bible is necessitated by its participation in cer-tain Enlightenment categories of thought. See George M. Marsden, *Fundamentalism and American Culture: The Shaping of Twentieth-Century Evangelicalism: 1870–1925* (New York: Oxford University Press, 1980). See also Bradley J. Longfield, *The Presbyterian Controversy: Fundamentalists, Modernists, and Moderates* (New York: Oxford University Press, 1991).

30. Niebuhr, *Christ and Culture*, 41.

31. *Ibid.*, 42.

32. *Ibid.*, 116.

33. David Penchansky, *The Politics of Biblical Theology* (Louisville: Westminster/John Knox Press, 1995), 12–15; Chopp, *Power to Speak*, 1–39 and 71–98; Michel Foucault, "Truth and Power," in *The Foucault Reader*, ed. Paul Rabinow (New York: Pantheon Books, 1984), 51–75. Even Niebuhr's employment of the term "center" de-centers the concept of "the church of the center." The centrist forms of church are the murkiest and messiest and least certain and are only "central" in that they stand next to others on a fluid continuum. They have no clear claim to make on a theological "Center"; they are merely between and in relation to others. Kathryn Tanner's analysis of Niebuhr is particularly trenchant in this context. She clearly per-

ceives the limitations of his concept of culture and the need for a Christ and culture analysis that recognizes that neither accommodation nor opposition and radical critique are the only options; the relationship between Christ and culture is always a mixture. Tanner, *Theories of Culture: A New Agenda for Theology* (Minneapolis: Fortress Press, 1997), 61–63, 117–19.

34. Niebuhr, *Christ and Culture*, 117–18.

35. *Ibid.*, 119.

36. *Ibid.*, 42.

37. *Ibid.*, 43. Reinhold Niebuhr expresses affinity with this type of ecclesiology, as when he writes: "Since man is a citizen of two worlds, he cannot afford to renounce his citizenship in either." *Does Civilization Need Religion? A Study in the Social Resources and Limitations of Religion in Modern Life* (New York: Macmillan, 1928), 186.

38. Niebuhr, *Christ and Culture*, 195–96.

39. *Ibid.*, 256.

40. *Ibid.*, 253.

41. It may seem inappropriate to compare Mead's taxonomy to the more rigorous academic offerings of Dulles and Niebuhr. One might regard it as a more appropriate project to analyze other academic approaches that make use of the idea of a "Christendom" model in their description of the conditions of contemporary Protestantism in North America. However, I have chosen to deal with Mead's taxonomy in this context for two reasons: (1) Mead provides an actual taxonomy divided into three paradigms ("Apostolic," "Christendom," and the coming paradigm), whereas others (like Douglas John Hall) seem to assume the fact of a "Christendom" model of the church without developing an actual taxonomy that includes other types; (2) while Mead's is not an academic taxonomy (and perhaps *because* it is not) it has emerged as an enormously influential theoretical construct among denominational professionals, pastors and other church leaders, some seminary teachers (especially in missiology and ministry), and theology students. Thus it should bear careful and critical examination.

42. Mead, *Once and Future Church*, 4.

43. *Ibid.*, v–vi.

44. *Ibid.*, vi, 8.

45. *Ibid.*, 7.

46. *Ibid.*, 8.

47. *Ibid.*, 9.

48. *Ibid.*, 9.

49. *Ibid.*, 8.

50. *Ibid.*, 8.

51. *Ibid.*, 9.

52. According to Lewis, not only is God iconoclastic, "[a]ll reality is iconoclastic." C. S. Lewis, *A Grief Observed* (New York: Seabury Press, 1961), 52.

53. Franz Overbeck cited in Karl Barth, *The Epistle to the Romans*, tr. Edwyn C. Hoskyns (Oxford: Oxford University Press, 1933), 3, note 2. Overbeck's influence on the early Karl Barth was profound.

54. Mead does, for instance, recognize the way in which "different styles and different structures emerged in different places" to carry out the church's tasks—the fact that "collegial and monarchical structures existed side by side" and that "communal experiments held sway in some places" in the first and second centuries, leading to what he describes as the Apostolic paradigm; the history, in fact, assumes a variety of attempts of the churches to ac-

commodate culture and to establish itself in its own place and time. Mead, *Once and Future Church,* 10.

55. For a helpful analysis of the theological diversity of early Christian communities, see David Rhoads, *The Challenge of Diversity: The Witness of Paul and the Gospels* (Minneapolis: Fortress Press, 1996), 1–13.

56. Mead, *Once and Future Church,* 10.

57. Acts 23:6.

58. Mead, *Once and Future Church,* 12. Consider, for instance, the contrasting and richly varied impressions of church, the varied understandings of world, of mission, of ministry, that arise from reflection on the *Epistles of Clement* and the *Epistles of Barnabas,* Polycarp's *Epistle* and the *Ignatian Letters,* the *Shepherd of Hermas* and the *Teaching of the Apostles,* Justin's *Apologies,* Irenaeus's *Against Heresies,* and the monumental Ante-Nicenes such as Tertullian and Origen.

59. Mead's work could have been enriched at this point by reference to Robert T. Handy's classic text, *A Christian America: Protestant Hopes and Historical Realities,* 2nd rev. ed. (New York: Oxford University Press, 1984); note also in this context Douglas John Hall's analysis of Constantinian "Christendom," especially in *Future of the Church*; in his monograph "An Awkward Church"; and in his "Remembered Voices, Neglected Words: The Unclaimed Legacy of 'Neo-Orthodoxy,'" Currie Lectures, Austin Presbyterian Theological Seminary, January 29–31, 1996. Handy's study contributed historical, and Hall's study theological, nuance to the notion of a quasi-Established or Christendom model of the church, though these ruminations continue also to flatten the church's experience in ways that more satisfactory typologies (like those of Dulles and Niebuhr) do not.

60. This situation has led some observers of the church to remark that in North America even the Roman Catholic Church is Protestant! Robert Bellah, in a recent address to the American Academy of Religion, remarked that he has come to believe that Roger Williams— not John Winthrop—is the defining figure for North American religious culture. Bellah, "Is There a Common American Culture?" address to the American Academy of Religion Annual Meeting, San Francisco, November 22, 1997. See also Robert N. Bellah, Richard Madsen, William M. Sullivan, Ann Swindler, and Steven Tipton, "Individualism and the Crisis of Civic Membership," *Christian Century,* May 8, 1996, 510–15, for a perspective on their research ten years after *Habits of the Heart.*

61. Hall also appreciates the heuristic value of using taxonomies in this manner, and he contributes significantly to this discussion in his allusion to Niebuhr's typology as a way of describing certain paradoxes and tensions within his understanding of a quasi-Established Church in Canada. *Future of the Church,* 3, 12–16.

62. Mead, *Once and Future Church,* 53–57.

63. Niebuhr, *Christ and Culture,* 231.

64. J. P. McEvoy, "Is Hawking Another Albert Einstein?" *Times* (London), October 23, 1995, 17.

65. Niebuhr, *Irony of American History,* viii.

66. Sebastian De Grazia's analysis of Renaissance Italian political and ecclesiastical conflicts is especially pertinent. *Machiavelli In Hell* (New York: Vintage, 1994), 3–122.

67. Kierkegaard's theological critique leveled at this form of state church in nineteenth-century Denmark continues to resonate among us (and to figure into the ecclesiological critique of theologians such as Hall); but here especially we need to be aware of paradoxical elements both in the particular manifestation of "Christendom" Kierkegaard criticized and his

criticism itself. And it is questionable how transferable this critique of the Danish state church is to the current ecclesiastical situation in North America, though some aspects of Kierkegaard's message appear dynamically analogous in certain respects. Note, for example, Kierkegaard's relationship to Bishop Mynster, as described in Walter Lowrie, *A Short Life of Kierkegaard* (Princeton: Princeton University Press, 1942), in light of the publication of Kierkegaard's *Training in Christianity* (Princeton: Princeton University Press, 1944); particularly consider his discussion of "Christendom," 37–39 and 108–18. See the following works of Kierkegaard: *Works of Love* (London: Oxford University Press, 1946), 194, and Douglas Steele's introduction, vii; *The Point of View* (Oxford: Oxford University Press, 1939), 138; and *Attack Upon "Christendom"* (Princeton: Princeton University Press, 1944); the supplement to the translator's introduction is valuable. See also David J. Gouwen's superb study, *Kierkegaard as Religious Thinker* (Cambridge: Cambridge University Press, 1996).

68. Michael Jinkins, "John Cotton and the Antinomian Controversy, 1636–1638: A Profile of Experiential Individualism in American Puritanism," *Scottish Journal of Theology* 43 (1990), no.3, 321–49. Note also John M. Murren's essay, "Religion and Politics in America from the First Settlements to the Civil War," in *Religion and American Politics: From the Colonial Period to the 1980s,* ed. Mark A. Noll (New York: Oxford University Press, 1990), 19–43.

69. Mead approvingly cites Stanley Hauerwas and William Willimon, *Resident Aliens* (Nashville: Abingdon, 1990).

70. Chopp, *Power to Speak,* 30–39. For Chopp, "the Word of creation and transformation" is the "perfectly open sign" that "opens out into its fullness, into the plentitude of its manifestation, into the multiplicity of language and discourse," bestowing meaning but also pointing "forward to new meanings with both specificity and solidarity" (30).

71. Karl Barth, *Church Dogmatics* II. 1. 61. Barth continues later in this passage: "Any other name is not the name of God. Any knowledge of any other name is not the knowledge of God. It is in this way and not another that God stands before man." Charles M. Wood cites this passage from Barth's *Dogmatics* in the context of noting how God cannot be objectified and grasped through our descriptions and categories, *Formation of Christian Understanding,* 35.

Four. Speaking of Church

1. Minear, *Images of the Church.*
2. Barth, *Church Dogmatics,* I. 1.23.
3. Samuel John Stone, "The Church's One Foundation," 1866.
4. As Stacy Johnson observes, specifically with reference to Karl Barth's interpretation of God's self-revelation: "The mystery of God" that is "'veiled' in the humanity of Jesus" is also "an unveiling, a hiddenness that discloses." William Stacy Johnson, *Karl Barth and the Postmodern Foundations of Theology* (Louisville: Westminster/John Knox Press, 1997), 129.
5. Dulles, *Models of the Church,* 32.
6. Minear, *Images of the Church,* 253.
7. Henry Chadwick, *The Early Church* (London: Penguin, 1967), 20.
8. Karl Barth, *Göttingen Dogmatics: Instruction in the Christian Religion,* tr. Geoffrey W. Bromiley, ed., Hannelotte Reiffen (Grand Rapids: Eerdmans, 1991), 23–24.
9. *Ibid.,* 24.
10. *Ibid.*
11. Compare Karl Barth, *Fides Quarens Intellectum: Anselms Beweis der Existenz Gottes im*

Zusammenhang seines theologischen Programms (Zollikon: Evangelischer, 1958), where Barth writes: "Und das Wort Christi ist identisch mit dem 'Wort der Christus Verkündigenden,' d.h. es ist legitim repräesentiert durch bestimmte Menschenworte" (21).

12. Barth, *Göttingen Dogmatics*, 24, 25.

13. As is raised in Hauerwas, "What Could It Mean for the Church to Be Christ's Body? A Question without a Clear Answer," to which I have already referred in another context. I would maintain that the question has no "clear answer" precisely because it is a false question. The church in the radical ambiguity and particularity of its human-divinity is the body of Christ. What does this mean? That is the question.

14. Roland Barthes, *Mythologies,* tr. Annette Lavers (New York: Hill and Wang, 1972), 74–75.

15. *Ibid.,* 75.

16. I introduce the neologism of phenomengnosis here to emphasize our attempts to understand the meaning of the rich ambiguities of life precisely in their ambiguity, in contrast to phenomenology, which holds (e.g., Husserl) that our proper goal is to gain access to the essence beyond the flux of ambiguous experience. A praxis-oriented discussion of phenomenology is presented in William F. Pinar and William M. Reynolds, *Understanding Curriculum as Phenomenological and Deconstructed Text* (New York: Columbia University Press, 1992), 1–91.

17. Barthes, *Mythologies,* 75–76.

18. *Ibid.,* 88. See also Barthes, *The Pleasure of the Text* (New York: Hill and Wang, 1975), 24–28.

19. Alan J. Torrance, introductory essay to *Christ, Justice and Peace: Toward a Theology of the State in Dialogue with the Barmen Declaration,* by Eberhard Jüngel, tr. D. Bruce Hamill and Alan J. Torrance (Edinburgh: T. and T. Clark, 1992), x.

20. Jüngel, *Christ, Justice, and Peace,* 67–73.

21. Calvin introduces this Pauline reflection in his refutation of Osiander. Calvin, *Institutes of the Christian Religion,* ed. John T. McNeill, tr. Ford Lewis Battles (Philadelphia: Westminster Press, 1960), 3.11.12.

22. Note Calvin, *Institutes,* 4.1.19–23.

23. T. E. Peck, *Notes on Ecclesiology* (Richmond, Va.: Presbyterian Committee of Publication, 1892), 8–9. As the title suggests, the book consists of class notes taken by Peck's students as he taught.

24. *Ibid.,* 9–22.

25. *Ibid.,* 14. Peck frankly places himself in that especially (but not exclusively) North American Protestant tradition that emphasizes voluntaristic joining over belonging, and thus places himself at tension with his larger Reformed ecclesiological tradition. In the following chapter I reflect specifically on the implications of this tension.

26. *Ibid.,* 20.

27. *Ibid.,* 20.

28. *Ibid.,* 21–22.

29. Barthes, *Mythologies,* 100–102.

30. *Ibid.,* 100.

31. *Ibid.,* 101.

32. *Ibid.,* 102.

33. Roland Barthes, *The Eiffel Tower and Other Mythologies,* tr. Richard Howard (New York: Farrar Straus Giroux, 1979).

34. *Ibid.*, 4.

35. *Ibid.*, 5.

36. *Ibid.*, 6–7.

37. *Ibid.*, 3.

38. *Ibid.*, 7.

39. St. Cyprian, Epistle "To the People, Concerning Five Schismatic Presbyters of the Faction of Felicissimus," in *The Ante-Nicene Fathers*, ed. Alexander Roberts and James Donaldson (Grand Rapids: Eerdmans, 1981), 5: 318.

40. Eberhard Jüngel, "The Church as Sacrament?" in *Theological Essays*, ed. and tr. J. B. Webster (Edinburgh: T. and T. Clark, 1989), 191–213.

41. *Ibid.*, 210.

42. *Ibid.*, 211.

43. See John Zizioulas, *Being as Communion: Studies in Personhood and the Church* (Crestwood, N.Y.: St. Vladimir's Seminary Press, 1985, 1997); and Torrance, *Persons in Communion.*

44. Jüngel, *Essays*, 206.

Five. Confessions

1. Staughton Lynd, ed., *Nonviolence in America: A Documentary History* (Indianapolis: Bobbs-Merrill, 1966), 477.

2. *Ibid.*, 477.

3. John Calvin, *Institutes*, 1.1.1.

4. Wittgenstein, *Culture and Value*, 17e.

5. Note, for instance, the manner in which Karl Barth reflects on Calvin's dictum: "Omnis recta cognitio Dei ab oboedientia nascitur," "True knowledge of God is born out of obedience". Barth, *Evangelical Theology: An Introduction*, tr. Grover Foley (Garden City, N.Y.: Anchor Books, 1964), 14.

6. Eberhard Busch, *Karl Barth: His Life from Letters and Autobiographical Texts*, 417.

7. Søren Kierkegaard, *Philosophical Fragments/Johannes Climacus*, ed. and tr. Howard V. Hong and Edna H. Hong (Princeton: Princeton University Press, 1985); the passage appears in *Johannes Climacus, or De Omnibus Dubitandum Est*, 134–135.

8. Perhaps no one writing in the field of theological reflection today has grasped this insight as well as Eberhard Jüngel, especially in his essay "Metaphorical Truth: Reflections on Theological Metaphor as a Contribution to a Hermeneutic of Narrative Theology," in his *Essays*, 16–71.

9. Reinhold Niebuhr, *Does Civilization Need Religion?* 186.

10. See Colin E. Gunton, *Theology through the Theologians: Selected Essays 1972–1995* (Edinburgh: T. and T. Clark, 1996), 151–68; also see Gunton, *Enlightenment and Alienation: An Essay towards a Trinitarian Theology* (Basingstoke, Hants: Marshall Morgan and Scott, 1985), 98–107.

11. To speak of Jesus Christ as transcendent in his humanity, we find ourselves speaking in different ways from the manner in which we discuss the transcendence of the second person of the trinity in the inner-life of God. Transcendence always signals otherness; but the otherness of Jesus Christ has forced us to engage in a single frame the otherness of God, the otherness of human particularity, and the otherness of death. But what do we mean by this birth being also a kind of death? Can we speak of this theologically, or are we limited to the poetic

magi of T. S. Eliot? When God entered into the dull round of existence, there was no way out but death. Even more, there was no way into this creaturely existence that was not an entrance also into death, death as change, as mutability, as corruption and decay of the flesh. This is the scandal of incarnation that provoked the reaction of Arius—and has provoked Arianism and Docetism in every age. To die is human, as it is to err. Unto this dying, the divine is born in Jesus Christ.

12. Robert Frost, "Kitty Hawk," in *The Poetry of Robert Frost* (New York: Holt, Rinehart and Winston, 1969), 434–35.

13. I cannot write these lines without being reminded of Dietrich Bonhoeffer's *Sanctorum Communio,* ed. Clifford J. Green, tr. Reinhard Krauss and Nancy Lukens (Minneapolis: Fortress Press, 1998). Note especially 208–82.

14. Jüngel, *Christ, Justice and Peace,* 70.

15. The sense in which I mean "systematic theology" is described aptly by Karl Barth; discussing the "juxtaposition of this noun and this adjective" ["systematic theology"] that is "based on a tradition which is quite recent and highly problematic," Barth continues: "Is not the term 'Systematic Theology' as paradoxical as a 'wooden iron'? One day this conception will disappear just as suddenly as it has come into being. Nevertheless, even if I allow myself to be called and to be a 'Professor of Systematic Theology,' I could never write a book under this title, as my great contemporary and colleague Tillich has done! A 'system' is an edifice of thought, constructed on certain fundamental conceptions which are selected in accordance with a certain philosophy by a method which corresponds to these conceptions. Theology cannot be carried on in confinement or under the pressure of such a construction. The subject of theology is the history of the communion of God with man and man with God. . . . The subject of theology is, in this sense, the 'Word of God.' Theology is a science and a teaching which *feels itself responsible* to the living command of this specific subject and to nothing else in heaven or on earth, in the choice of its methods, its questions and answers, its concepts and language, its goals and limitations. Theology is a free science because it is based on and determined by the kingly freedom of the word of God; for that very reason it can never be 'Systematic Theology.'" Karl Barth, foreword to *Dogmatics in Outline,* tr. G. T. Thomson (New York: Harper and Row, 1959), 5. This foreword did not appear in the earlier edition of the English translation (London: Student Christian Movement Press, 1949).

16. I use the term "ecclesial" here in contrast to the way Peter C. Hodgson uses it in his *Re-visioning the Church.* While Hodgson uses the term to introduce a tension between "the ideal, distinctive or essential features of the Christian church" and "the actual historical manifestations of Christianity," I want to stress the fact that there is no such essential-existential dichotomy. The church that exists is ecclesial; and that which is ecclesial is "the empirical, historical, institutional reality" (27). The church is judged not by comparison to an essential ideal but by its response to the call of God, by its baptism into the baptism of the Christ in concrete historical reality. Notwithstanding this critique, Hodgson's book is one of the most interesting and provocative books in the field of ecclesiology.

17. Denham Grierson, *Transforming a People of God* (Melbourne, Australia: Joint Board of Christian Education, 1984), 36. Grierson goes on to say: "If faith is to give birth to deepened awareness and transforming power in the lives of the people it must learn to name itself in its local, particular taken-for-granted reality."

18. Karl Rahner's *Theological Investigations,* for instance, are paradigmatic occasional theological reflections.

19. For instance, Paula Cooey, *Family, Freedom, and Faith: Building Community Today* (Louisville: Westminster/John Knox Press, 1996).

20. See, for example, William J. Bouwsma, *John Calvin: A Sixteenth Century Portrait* (New York: Oxford University Press, 1988); Ford Lewis Battles, *Interpreting John Calvin*, ed. Robert Benedetto (Grand Rapids: Baker Books, 1996); T. H. L. Parker, *John Calvin: A Biography* (Philadelphia: Westminster Press, 1975); Alister E. McGrath, *A Life of John Calvin: A Study in the Shaping of Western Culture* (Oxford: Basil Blackwell, 1990).

21. George S. Hendry, "Christology," in *A Dictionary of Christian Theology*, ed. Alan Richardson (Philadelphia: Westminster Press, 1969), 52. This article is, in my opinion, the best summary of the historical development of the doctrine of Christology written.

22. Note T. F. Torrance's study of the doctrine of the Christ in his *Trinitarian Faith*, 110–90.

23. Hendry, "Christology," 52.

24. Emil Brunner, *The Christian Doctrine of Creation and Redemption: Dogmatics*, tr. Olive Wyon (Philadelphia: Westminster Press, 1952), 2: 322. Hendry also quotes Brunner in support ("Christology," 53).

25. Paul Althaus, *The Theology of Martin Luther* (Philadelphia: Fortress Press, 1966); Alister E. McGrath, *Luther's Theology of the Cross* (Oxford: Basil Blackwell, 1985). During the Heidelberg Disputation of April 1518, Luther said: "[H]e deserves to be called a theologian ... who comprehends the visible and manifest things of God through the suffering and the cross ... true theology and recognition of God are in the crucified Christ." E. G. Rupp and Benjamin Drewery, *Martin Luther* (London: Edward Arnold, 1970), 28–29. Peter Taylor Forsyth, *The Person and Place of Jesus Christ* (London: Independent Press, 1909) and *The Work of Christ* (London: Independent Press, 1910); Jürgen Moltmann, *The Crucified God: The Cross of Christ as the Foundation and Criticism of Christian Theology* (New York: Harper and Row, 1973). See also Michael Jinkins and Stephen Breck Reid, "John McLeod Campbell on Christ's Cry of Dereliction: A Case Study in Trinitarian Hermeneutics," *EQ: The Evangelical Quarterly* 70 (1998), no. 2, 135–49.

26. Edward Schillebeeckx, *The Church with a Human Face: A New and Expanded Theology of Ministry*, tr. John Bowden (New York: Crossroad, 1990), 5.

27. Dietrich Bonhoeffer, *Christ the Center*, tr. John Bowden (New York: Harper and Row, 1960), 29.

28. Jacques Derrida's essay "*Cogito* and the History of Madness" makes fascinating (point/counter-point) reading in relation to Bonhoeffer's theological reflections (in *Writing and Difference*, 31–63). Derrida is in dialogue in this essay with Descartes, as is apparent from the title, but also with Michel Foucault, *Madness and Civilization: A History of Insanity in the Age of Reason*, tr. Richard Howard (New York: Random House, 1965).

29. Bonhoeffer, *Christ the Center*, 27.

30. *Ibid.*, 30.

31. *Ibid.*, 31.

32. Paul Tillich, *Systematic Theology*, vol. 2, *Existence and the Christ* (Chicago: University of Chicago, 1957), 13. Compare David Tracy's extremely helpful analysis of a "model of correlation," with respect to Tillich, of course, but also (and more profitably) with respect to Schillebeeckx's "mutually critical correlations," in *The Analogical Imagination: Christian Theology and the Culture of Pluralism* (New York: Crossroad, 1981), 47–98, especially p. 88 note 44. Here Tracy observes that "any theologian who has interpretations of two distinct phenomena (tradition and situation) must somehow correlate those interpretations: whether through claims for

identity, radical nonidentity, similarities, continuities or analogies. . . . Even Barthians correlate, if only ordinarily in the form of *Nein*, to the extra-theological interpretations of the situation!" Barth's own homiletical thought indicates a more positive concern for (though not a method-ology to address) "correlation" in his early and frequently cited in "The Need of Christian Preaching," in *Das Wort Gottes und die Theologie* (Munich: Christian Kaiser, 1925), English translation, *The Word of God and the Word of Man*, tr. Douglas Horton (Gloucester: Peter Smith, 1978). (Unfortunately Horton's translation is not entirely adequate, thus I shall trans-late.) Barth articulates the preacher's problem: "Zu den menschen, in den unerhörten Wider-spruch ihres Lebens hinein sollte ich ja als Pfarrer reden, aber reden von der nicht minder unerhörten Botschaft der Bibel, die diesem Widerspruch des Lebens als ein neues Rätsel gegenübersteht." ("As a minister I should speak to *people* in the shocking contradiction of their life, but to speak the no less shocking message of the Bible, the contradictions of which are as much a riddle as life.") Barth confesses that he has found no way out of this "critical situation"; rather, the situation is itself, for him, "the reality of *all* theology." Theology, Barth writes, is "the description of an embarrassment," that is, an unresolvable problem thrust upon us by our ex-istence and the Word of God. (These passages are found on pp. 101–2 of the 1925 Munich edi-tion.) Thus Barth engages in the struggle of theological correlation—especially when his theo-logical reflection is grounded in the existential situation of the preacher—but is wary of methodologies that might rescue the theologian from the embarrassment of the critical situa-tion. Barth's unwillingness to throw the drowning preacher a methodological rope can be con-strued as a word of liberation because any methodology that might deliver us carries for Barth the force of idolatry. Such methodology is an attempt to circumvent the crisis of radical faith in the God who meets us under the sign of contradiction. See also Barth, *Göttingen Dogmatics*, 1: 23–41. Scott Black Johnston understands Barth well, especially at this point in Barth's theolog-ical development and in the context of post-modern homiletical theory; see Ronald J. Allen, Barbara Shires Blaisdell, and Scott Black Johnston, *Theology for Preaching: Authority, Truth and Knowledge of God in a Postmodern Ethos* (Nashville: Abingdon Press, 1997), 27–33. Note also in this context David Tracy, *Blessed Rage for Order: The New Pluralism in Theology* (New York: Crossroad, 1978), comparatively with *Plurality and Ambiguity: Hermeneutics, Religion, Hope* (San Francisco, 1987). See also Kathryn Tanner, *Theories of Culture: A New Agenda for Theology* (Minneapolis: Fortress Press, 1997), 65–69.

33. Bonhoeffer, *Christ the Center*, 32. Bonhoeffer's approach lays an axe to the trunk of christological foundationalism. There is no security in the confrontation with Jesus Christ. The community of faith exists by virtue of the faith created in it in the encounter with Christ.

34. Note particularly Dulles, *Models of the Church*, 34–102.

35. The hermeneutical nature of this task is clearly seen in Wood, *Formation of Christian Understanding*, 15–49.

36. Von Balthasar, *Church and World*, 115.

37. Niebuhr, *The Irony of American History*, viii. "The ironic situation," Niebuhr adds, "is distinguished from a pathetic one by the fact that the person involved in it bears some re-sponsibility for it. It is differentiated from tragedy by the fact that the responsibility is related to an unconscious weakness rather than to a conscious resolution."

38. Calvin, *Institutes*, 4.1.10.

39. Augsburg Confession, Articles of Faith and Doctrine, VII. [The Church], in *The Book of Conford: the Confessions of the Evangelical Lutheran Church*, ed. and tr. Theodore G. Tap-pert, Jaroslav Pelikan, Robert H. Fischer, and Arthur C. Piepkorn (Philadelphia: Muhlenberg Press, 1959).

40. Calvin, *Institutes*, 4.1.10.

41. John Locke, "A Letter Concerning Toleration," in *On Politics and Education* (New York: Walter J. Black, 1947), 27–28.

42. I examine Edwards's thought in greater detail in " 'The Being of Beings': Jonathan Edwards' Understanding of God As Reflected in His Final Treatises," *Scottish Journal of Theology* 46 (1993), no. 2, 161–90, and in "The 'True Remedy': Jonathan Edwards' Soteriological Perspective As Observed in His Revival Treatises," *Scottish Journal of Theology* 48 (1995), no. 2, 185–209.

43. Luke Timothy Johnson, "Debate and Discernment: Scripture and the Spirit," *Commonweal*, January 28, 1994, 11.

44. David H. Kelsey, *To Understand God Truly: What's Theological about Theological Schools* (Louisville: Westminster/John Knox Press, 1992), 32.

45. An interesting version of this view is put forward in Don S. Browning, *A Fundamental Practical Theology: Descriptive and Strategic Proposals* (Minneapolis: Fortress Press, 1991).

46. The pastor-theologian who wants to enter seriously upon this work has many good resources today. Methodological introductions include such general resources in ethnography as James P. Spradley, *The Ethnographic Interview* (New York: Holt, Rinehart and Winston, 1979) and Spradley's companion volume *The Participant Observer* (1979) and introductions to the use of ethnographic and theological-sociological methods in congregations such as Melvin D. William's study "The Conflict of Corporate Church and Spiritual Community: An Ethnographic Analysis," in *Building Effective Ministry*, ed. Carl S. Dudley (San Francisco: Harper and Row, 1983), 55–67; and Jackson W. Carroll, Carl S. Dudley, and William McKinney, eds., *Handbook for Congregational Studies* (Nashville: Abingdon Press, 1986). Arguably the best complete model for doing congregational study is Grierson, *Transforming A People of God*. See also Robert J. Schreiter, *Constructing Local Theologies* (Maryknoll, N.Y.: Orbis Books, 1994); Jose Miguez Bonino, *Doing Theology in a Revolutionary Situation* (Philadelphia: Fortress Press, 1975), chapters 5–8; and Clodovis Boff, *Theology and Praxis: Epistemological Foundations*, tr. Robert R. Barr (Maryknoll, N.Y.: Orbis Books, 1987. Examples of attempts to take seriously the description of the particular congregation vary greatly in their ability to do theological reflection. Notable publications in this area include: Samuel G. Freedman, *Upon This Rock: The Miracles of a Black Church* (New York: HarperCollins, 1993); James P. Wind, *Places of Worship* (Nashville: American Association for State and Local History, 1990); James P. Wind and James W. Lewis, eds., *American Congregations*, vol. 1, *Portraits of Twelve Religious Communites* (Chicago: University of Chicago Press, 1994); especially note Wayne Flynt's chapter, " 'A Special Feeling of Closeness': Mt. Hebron Baptist Church, Leeds, Alabama," 103–58; and Jeff Todd Titon, *Powerhouse for God: Speech, Chant, and Song in an Appalachian Baptist Church* (Austin: University of Texas Press, 1988).

47. Avery Dulles, *The Craft of Theology: From Symbol to System* (New York: Crossroad, 1992), 17–24.

Epilogue

1. While this characterization of Berlin is in need of considerable nuance, it can stand in this context. See Isaiah Berlin, *Against the Current: Essays in the History of Ideas,* ed. Henry Hardy (London: Hogarth Press, 1979; London: Pimlico Press, 1997); *The Crooked Timber of Humanity,* ed. Henry Hardy (New York: Knopf, 1991); *The Sense of Reality: Studies in Ideas and*

Their History, ed. Henry Hardy (New York: Farrar Straus Giroux, 1996); *The Proper Study of Mankind: An Anthology of Essays* (London: Pimlico Press, 1998). See also John Gray, *Isaiah Berlin* (London: HarperCollins, 1995), 5–75, particularly where Gray discusses this issue (22).

2. Mark C. Taylor, *Erring: A Postmodern A/theology* (Chicago: University of Chicago Press, 1984), 6.

3. *Ibid.,* 176–77. Also see Scott Black Johnston's illuminating reflections with reference to Taylor in Allen, Blaisdell, and Johnston, *Theology for Preaching,* 74.

Select Bibliography

Books and Dissertations

Allen, Ronald J., Barbara Shires Blaisdell, and Scott Black Johnston. *Theology for Preaching: Authority, Truth and Knowledge of God in a Postmodern Ethos*. Nashville: Abingdon Press, 1997.

Althaus, Paul. *The Theology of Martin Luther*. Philadelphia: Fortress Press, 1966.

Aristotle. *The Politics*. Ed. Stephen Everson. Cambridge: Cambridge University Press, 1988.

Augustine. *Confessions*. Tr. Henry Chadwick. Oxford: Oxford University Press, 1991.

Balthasar, Hans Urs von. *Church and World*. Tr. A. V. Littledale and Alexander Dru. New York: Herder and Herder, 1967.

Barth, Karl. *Göttingen Dogmatics: Instruction in the Christian Religion*. Tr. Geoffrey W. Bromiley. Ed. Hannelotte Reiffen. Grand Rapids: Eerdmans, 1991.

———. *Church Dogmatics*. Ed. Geoffrey W. Bromiley and Thomas F. Torrance. Edinburgh: T. and T. Clark, 1936–1975.

———. *Learning Jesus Christ through the Heidelberg Catechism*. Tr. Shirley C. Guthrie. Grand Rapids: Eerdmans, 1964.

———. *Evangelical Theology: An Introduction*. Tr. Grover Foley. Garden City, N.Y.: Anchor Books, 1964.

———. *Dogmatik im Grundriss*. Zollikon: Christian Kaiser/Evangelischer, 1947. English translation: *Dogmatics in Outline*. Tr. G. T. Thomson. New York: Harper and Row, 1959.

———. *Fides Quarens Intellectum: Anselms Beweis der Existenz Gottes im Zusammenhang seines theologischen Programms*. Zollikon: Evangelischer, 1958.

———. *The Epistle to the Romans*. Tr. Edwyn C. Hoskyns. Oxford: Oxford University Press, 1933.

———. *Das Wort Gottes und die Theologie*. Munich: Christian Kaiser, 1925. English translation: *The Word of God and the Word of Man*. Tr. Douglas Horton. Gloucester: Peter Smith, 1978.

Barth, Marcus. *Ephesians 1–3*. Anchor Bible Commentary. Garden City, N.Y.: Doubleday, 1979.

Barthes, Roland. *Criticism and Truth*. Tr. Katrine Pilcher Keuneman. Minneapolis: University of Minnesota Press, 1987.

———. *The Eiffel Tower and Other Mythologies*. Tr. Richard Howard. New York: Farrar Straus Giroux, 1979.

———. *The Pleasure of the Text*. New York: Hill and Wang, 1975.

————. *Mythologies.* Tr. Annette Lavers. New York: Hill and Wang, 1972.

Bateson, Gregory. *Steps to an Ecology of Mind.* Northvale, N.J.: Jacob Aronson, 1987.

Battles, Ford Lewis. *Interpreting John Calvin.* Ed. Robert Benedetto. Grand Rapids: Baker Books, 1996.

Bellah, Robert N., Richard Madsen, William M. Sullivan, Ann Swindler, and Steven M. Tipton. *Habits of the Heart: Individualism and Commitment in American Life.* Berkeley: University of California Press, 1985.

Benedict of Nursia. *The Rule of St. Benedict.* Tr. David Parry. London: Darton Longman and Todd, 1984.

Berlin, Isaiah. *The Proper Study of Mankind: An Anthology of Essays.* London: Pimlico Press, 1998.

————. *Against the Current: Essays in the History of Ideas.* Ed. Henry Hardy. London: Hogarth Press, 1979; London: Pimlico Press, 1997.

————. *The Sense of Reality: Studies in Ideas and Their History.* Ed. Henry Hardy. New York: Farrar Straus Giroux, 1996.

————. *The Crooked Timber of Humanity.* Ed. Henry Hardy. New York: Knopf, 1991.

Berrier, Floyd L. "A New Context for Doing United Methodist Theology." Columbia Theological Seminary, Decatur, Ga., dissertation, 1990.

Boff, Clodovis. *Theology and Praxis: Epistemological Foundations.* Tr. Robert R. Barr. Maryknoll, N.Y.: Orbis Books, 1987.

Bonhoeffer, Dietrich. *Sanctorum Communio.* Ed. Clifford J. Green, tr. Reinhard Krauss and Nancy Lukens (Minneapolis: Fortress Press, 1998).

————. *The Cost of Discipleship.* Rev. ed. New York: Macmillan, 1963.

————. *Christ the Center.* Tr. John Bowden. New York: Harper and Row, 1960.

Bonino, Jose Miguez. *Doing Theology in a Revolutionary Situation.* Philadelphia: Fortress Press, 1975.

Bouwsma, William J. *John Calvin: A Sixteenth Century Portrait.* New York: Oxford University Press, 1988.

Bradley, Ian. *Marching to the Promised Land: Has the Church a Future?* London: John Murray, 1992.

Browning, Don S. *A Fundamental Practical Theology: Descriptive and Strategic Proposals.* Minneapolis: Fortress Press, 1991.

Brunner, Emil. *The Christian Doctrine of Creation and Redemption.* Vol. 2. *Dogmatics.* Tr. Olive Wyon. Philadelphia: Westminster Press, 1952.

Busch, Eberhard. *Karl Barth: His Life from Letters and Autobiographical Texts.* Tr. John Bowden. Philadelphia: Fortress Press, 1975.

Calvin, John. *Institutes of the Christian Religion.* Ed. John T. McNeill. Tr. Ford Lewis Battles. Philadelphia: Westminster Press, 1960.

Caputo, John D. *The Prayers and Tears of Jacques Derrida: Religion without Religion.* Bloomington: Indiana University Press, 1997.

Carothers, J. Edward. *The Paralysis of Mainstream Protestant Leadership.* Nashville: Abingdon Press, 1990.

Carroll, Jackson W., Carl S. Dudley, and William McKinney, eds. *Handbook for Congregational Studies.* Nashville: Abingdon Press, 1986.

Chadwick, Henry. *The Early Church.* London: Penguin, 1967.

Chesterton, G. K. *The Everlasting Man*. London: Hodder and Stoughton, 1925.

———. *Orthodoxy*. London: Bodley Head, 1908.

Chopp, Rebecca. *The Power to Speak: Feminism, Language, God*. New York: Crossroad, 1992.

Chun, Sang Eui. "A Praxis Credo: A Practical Evangelism Model from a Comparative Study of the Korean Methodist Church and the United Methodist Church." Saint Paul School of Theology, Kansas City, Missouri, dissertation, 1994.

Coalter, Milton J., and Virgil Cruz, eds. *How Shall We Witness?* Louisville: Westminster/John Knox Press, 1995.

Coalter, Milton J., John M. Mulder, and Louis B. Weeks, eds. *The Organizational Revolution: Presbyterians and American Denominationalism*. Louisville: Westminster/John Knox, 1992.

———. *The Confessional Mosaic: Presbyterians and Twentieth-Century Theology*. Louisville: Westminster/John Knox, 1990.

———. *The Mainstream Protestant "Decline": The Presbyterian Pattern*. Louisville: Westminster/John Knox, 1990.

———. *The Diversity of Discipleship: Presbyterians and Twentieth-Century Christian Witness*. Louisville: Westminster/John Knox, 1991.

———. *The Pluralistic Vision: Presbyterians and Mainstream Protestant Education and Leadership*. Louisville: Westminster/John Knox, 1992.

———. *The Presbyterian Predicament: Six Perspectives*. Louisville: Westminster/John Knox, 1992.

———. *The Re-Forming Tradition: Presbyterians and Mainstream Protestantism*. Louisville: Westminster/John Knox, 1992.

Cooey, Paula. *Family, Freedom, and Faith: Building Community Today*. Louisville: Westminster/John Knox Press, 1996.

Craddock, Fred. *Preaching*. Nashville: Abingdon Press, 1985.

Davis, Colin. *Levinas*. Notre Dame: University of Notre Dame Press, 1996.

De Grazia, Sebastian. *Machiavelli in Hell*. New York: Vintage, 1994.

Derrida, Jacques. *The Gift of Death*. Tr. David Wills. Chicago: University of Chicago Press, 1995.

———. *Of Spirit: Heidegger and the Question*. Tr. Geoffrey Bennington and Rachel Bowlby. Chicago: University of Chicago Press, 1989.

———. *Writing and Difference*. Tr. Alan Bass. Chicago: University of Chicago Press, 1978.

———. *Speech and Phenomena: And Other Essays on Husserl's Theory of Signs*. Tr. David B. Allison. Evanston: Northwestern University Press, 1973.

Dostoyevsky, Fyodor. *The Brothers Karamazov*. Tr. Constance Garnett. Ed. Manuel Komroff. New York: New American Library, 1957.

Dudley, Carl S., ed. *Building Effective Ministry*. San Francisco: Harper and Row, 1983.

Dulles, Avery. *The Craft of Theology: From Symbol to System*. New York: Crossroad, 1992.

———. *Models of the Church*. New York: Doubleday; 1st ed. 1978; expanded ed. 1987.

Eco, Umberto. *The Role of the Reader: Explorations in the Semiotics of Texts*. Bloomington: Indiana University Press, 1979.

Forsyth, Peter Taylor. *The Work of Christ*. London: Independent Press, 1910.

———. *The Person and Place of Jesus Christ*. London: Independent Press, 1909.

Foucault, Michel. *Madness and Civilization: A History of Insanity in the Age of Reason*. Tr. Richard Howard. New York: Vintage Books, 1988.

————. *The Foucault Reader*. Ed. Paul Rabinow. New York: Pantheon Books, 1984.

Freedman, Samuel G. *Upon This Rock: The Miracles of a Black Church*. New York: Harper-Collins, 1993.

Frost, Robert. *The Poetry of Robert Frost*. New York: Holt, Rinehart and Winston, 1969.

Giakalis, Ambrosios. *Images of the Divine: The Theology of Icons at the Seventh Ecumenical Council*. Leiden: E. J. Brill, 1994.

Gouwen, David J. *Kierkegaard as Religious Thinker*. Cambridge: Cambridge University Press, 1996.

Gray, John. *Isaiah Berlin*. London: HarperCollins, 1995.

Grierson, Denham. *Transforming a People of God*. Melbourne, Australia: Joint Board of Christian Education, 1984.

Gunton, Colin E. *The Triune Creator: A Historical and Systematic Study*. Grand Rapids: Eerdmans, 1998.

————. *Theology through the Theologians: Selected Essays, 1972–1995*. Edinburgh: T. and T. Clark, 1996.

————. *The One, the Three and the Many: God, Creation and the Culture of Modernity. The 1992 Bampton Lectures*. Cambridge: Cambridge University Press, 1993.

————. *The Promise of Trinitarian Theology*. Edinburgh: T. and T. Clark, 1991.

————. *Enlightenment and Alienation: An Essay towards a Trinitarian Theology*. Basingstoke, Hants: Marshall Morgan and Scott, 1985.

Gutmann, Joseph, ed. *The Image and the Word: Confrontations in Judaism, Christianity and Islam*. Missoula, Mont.: Scholars Press, 1977.

Hall, Douglas John. *The Future of the Church: Where Are We Headed?* N.p.: United Church of Canada Publishing House, 1989.

Handy, Robert T. *A Christian America: Protestant Hopes and Historical Realities*. 2nd Rev. Ed. New York: Oxford University Press, 1984.

Hauerwas, Stanley. *In Good Company: The Church as Polis*. Notre Dame: University of Notre Dame, 1995.

Hauerwas, Stanley, and William Willimon. *Resident Aliens*. Nashville: Abingdon Press, 1990.

Havel, Václav. *Open Letters: Selected Writings, 1965–1990*. Ed. Paul Wilson. New York: Vintage Books, 1992.

————. *Summer Meditations*. New York: Knopf, 1992.

Hawking, Stephen. *A Brief History of Time: From the Big Bang to Black Holes*. London: Bantam, 1988.

Heidegger, Martin. *Being and Time*. Tr. John Macquarrie and Edward Robinson. Oxford: Basil Blackwell, 1962.

Hodgson, Peter. *Revisioning the Church: Ecclesial Freedom in the New Paradigm*. Minneapolis: Fortress Press, 1988.

Jay, Eric G. *The Church: Its Changing Image through Twenty Centuries*. 2 vols. London: SPCK, 1977, 1978.

Jinkins, Michael. *In the House of the Lord: Inhabiting the Psalms of Lament*. Collegeville, Minn.: Liturgical Press, 1998.

Jinkins, Michael, and Deborah Bradshaw Jinkins. *The Character of Leadership: Political Realism and Public Virtue in Nonprofit Organizations*. San Francisco: Jossey-Bass, 1998.

————. *Power and Change in Parish Ministry*. Washington, D.C.: Alban Institute, 1991.

John of Damascus. *On Divine Images: Three Apologies against Those Who Attack the Divine Images.* Tr. David Anderson. Crestwood, N.Y.: St. Vladimir's Seminary Press, 1980.

Johnson, William Stacy. *Karl Barth and the Postmodern Foundations of Theology.* Louisville: Westminster/John Knox Press, 1997.

Jüngel, Eberhard. *Christ, Justice and Peace: Toward a Theology of the State in Dialogue with the Barmen Declaration.* Tr. D. Bruce Hamill and Alan J. Torrance. Edinburgh: T. and T. Clark, 1992.

———. *Theological Essays.* Ed. and tr. J. B. Webster. Edinburgh: T. and T. Clark, 1989.

———. *God as the Mystery of the World: On the Foundation of Theology of the Crucified One in the Dispute between Theism and Atheism.* Tr. Darrell L. Guder. Grand Rapids: Eerdmans, 1983.

Keck, Leander E. *The Church Confident.* Nashville: Abingdon Press, 1983.

Kelsey, David H. *To Understand God Truly: What's Theological about Theological Schools.* Louisville: Westminster/John Knox Press, 1992.

Kierkegaard, Søren. *Philosophical Fragments/ Johannes Climacus.* Ed. and tr. Howard V. Hong and Edna H. Hong. Princeton: Princeton University Press, 1985.

———. *Works of Love.* Tr. David F. Swenson and Lillian Marvin Swenson. London: Oxford University Press, 1946.

———. *Attack upon "Christendom": 1854–1855.* Tr. Walter Lowrie. Princeton: Princeton University Press, 1944.

———. *Training in Christianity.* Tr. Walter Lowrie. Princeton: Princeton University Press, 1944.

———. *The Point of View.* Tr. Walter Lowrie. Oxford: Oxford University Press, 1939.

Kittel, Gerhard. *Theological Dictionary of the New Testament.* Ed. and tr. Geoffrey W. Bromiley. 10 vols. Grand Rapids: Eerdmans, 1964.

Levinas, Emmanuel. *Basic Philosophical Writings.* Ed. Andriaan T. Peperzak, Simon Critchley, and Robert Bernasconi. Bloomington: Indiana University Press, 1996.

———. *The Levinas Reader.* Tr. Seán Hand. Oxford: Blackwell, 1989.

Lévi-Strauss, Claude. *Tristes Tropiques: An Anthropological Study of Primitive Societies in Brazil.* New York: Atheneum, 1969.

Lewis, C. S. *A Grief Observed.* New York: Seabury Press, 1961.

Locke, John. *On Politics and Education.* New York: Walter J. Black, 1947.

Longfield, Bradley J. *The Presbyterian Controversy: Fundamentlists, Modernists, and Moderates.* New York: Oxford University Press, 1991.

Lowe, Walter. *Theology and Difference: The Wound of Reason.* Bloomington: Indiana University Press, 1993.

Lowrie, Walter. *A Short Life of Kierkegaard.* Princeton: Princeton University Press, 1942.

Lynd, Staughton, ed. *Nonviolence in America: A Documentary History.* Indianapolis: Bobbs-Merrill, 1966.

McGrath, Alister E. *A Life of John Calvin: A Study in the Shaping of Western Culture.* Oxford: Basil Blackwell, 1990.

———. *Luther's Theology of the Cross.* Oxford: Basil Blackwell, 1985.

Macmurray, John. *Persons In Relation.* London: Faber and Faber, 1961; new ed. 1991.

Mansfield, Harvey C. *Machiavelli's Virtue.* Chicago: University of Chicago Press, 1996.

Marney, Carlyle. *Priests to Each Other.* Valley Forge: Judson Press, 1974.

Marsden, George M. *Fundamentalism and American Culture: The Shaping of Twentieth-Century Evangelicalism: 1870–1925.* New York: Oxford University Press, 1980.

Mead, Loren. *The Once and Future Church: Reinventing the Congregation for a New Mission Frontier.* Washington D.C.: Alban Institute, 1991.

Meeks, Donald E. *The Scottish Highlands: The Churches and Gaelic Culture.* Geneva: World Council of Churches Publications, 1996.

Meredith, Anthony. *The Cappadocians.* Crestwood, N.Y.: St. Vladimir's Seminary Press, 1995.

Miller, Donald E. *Reinventing American Protestantism: Christianity in the New Millennium.* Berkeley: University of California Press, 1997.

Minear, Paul. *Images of the Church in the New Testament.* Philadelphia: Westminster Press, 1960.

Moltmann, Jürgen. *The Crucified God: The Cross of Christ as the Foundation and Criticism of Christian Theology.* New York: Harper and Row, 1973.

Murray, James A. H., et al. eds. *The Compact Oxford English Dictionary.* 2nd ed. Oxford: Oxford University Press, 1991.

Niebuhr, H. Richard. *The Responsible Self: An Essay in Christian Moral Philosophy.* New York: Harper and Row, 1963.

———. *Christ and Culture.* New York: Harper and Row, 1951.

Niebuhr, Reinhold. *The Irony of American History.* New York: Scribner's, 1952.

———. *Moral Man and Immoral Society.* New York: Scribner's, 1932.

———. *Does Civilization Need Religion? A Study in the Social Resources and Limitations of Religion in Modern Life.* New York: Macmillan, 1928.

Noll, Mark A. ed. *Religion and American Politics: From the Colonial Period to the 1980s.* New York: Oxford University Press, 1990.

Norris, Christopher. *Derrida.* Cambridge: Harvard University Press, 1987.

Norris, Kathleen. *The Cloister Walk.* New York: Riverhead Books, 1963.

Parker, T. H. L. *John Calvin: A Biography.* Philadelphia: Westminster Press, 1975.

Peck, T. E. *Notes on Ecclesiology.* Richmond, Va.: Presbyterian Committee of Publication, 1892.

Pelikan, Jaroslav. *Imago Dei: The Byzantine Apologia for Icons.* Princeton: Princeton University Press, 1990.

Penchansky, David. *The Politics of Biblical Theology.* Louisville: Westminster/John Knox Press, 1995.

Pinar, William F., and William M. Reynolds. *Understanding Curriculum as Phenomenological and Deconstructed Text.* New York: Columbia University Press, 1992.

Rhoads, David. *The Challenge of Diversity: The Witness of Paul and the Gospels.* Minneapolis: Fortress Press, 1996.

Richardson, Alan. *Dictionary of Christian Theology.* Philadelphia: Westminster Press, 1969.

Ricoeur, Paul. *Figuring the Sacred: Religion, Narrative and Imagination.* Tr. David Pellauer. Ed. Mark I. Wallace. Minneapolis: Fortress Press, 1995.

———. *Oneself as Another.* Tr. Kathleen Blamey. Chicago: University of Chicago Press, 1992.

Roberts, Alexander, and James Donaldson. *The Ante-Nicene Fathers.* Grand Rapids: Eerdmans, 1980.

Rupp, E. G., and Benjamin Drewery. *Martin Luther.* London: Edward Arnold, 1970.

Schaff, Philip, and Henry Wace, eds. *Nicene and Post-Nicene Fathers of the Christian Church.* Second series. Grand Rapids: Eerdmans, 1983.

Schillebeeckx, Edward. *The Church: The Human Story of God.* Tr. John Bowden. New York: Crossroad, 1990.

——. *The Church with a Human Face: A New and Expanded Theology of Ministry.* Tr. John Bowden. New York: Crossroad, 1990.

Schleiermacher, Friedrich. *The Christian Faith.* Ed. H. R. Macintosh. Tr. James S. Stewart. Edinburgh: T. and T. Clark, 1928.

Schlesinger, Arthur M., Jr. *The Cycles of American History.* Boston: Houghton Mifflin, 1986.

Schreiter, Robert J. *Constructing Local Theologies.* Maryknoll, N.Y.: Orbis Books, 1994.

Schweizer, Eduard. *Lordship and Discipleship.* London: SCM Press, 1960.

Shipley, Joseph T. *Dictionary of Word Origins.* New York: Philosophical Library, 1945.

Spradley, James P. *The Participant Observer.* New York: Holt, Rinehart and Winston, 1979.

——. *The Ethnographic Interview.* New York: Holt, Rinehart and Winston, 1979.

Stendahl, Krister. *Final Account: Paul's Letter to the Romans.* Minneapolis: Fortress Press, 1995.

Stringfellow, William. *A Keeper of the Word: Selected Writings of William Stringfellow.* Ed. Bill Wylie Kellerman. Grand Rapids: Eerdmans, 1994.

——. *A Simplicity of Faith: My Experience in Mourning.* Nashville: Abingdon Press, 1982.

——. *Instead of Death.* Rev. ed. New York: Seabury Press, 1976.

Tanner, Kathryn. *Theories of Culture: A New Agenda for Theology.* Minneapolis: Fortress Press, 1997.

Tappert, Theodore G., Jaroslav Pelikan, Robert H. Fischer, and Arthur C. Piepkorn. *The Book of Concord: The Confessions of the Evangelical Lutheran Church.* Philadelphia: Muhlenberg Press, 1959.

Tavener, John, and Mother Thekla. *Ikons: Meditations in Words and Music.* London: Fount, 1995.

Taylor, Mark C. *Erring: A Postmodern A/theology.* Chicago: University of Chicago Press, 1984.

Tillich, Paul. *Systematic Theology.* Vol. 2. *Existence and the Christ.* Chicago: University of Chicago Press, 1957.

Titon, Jeff Todd. *Powerhouse for God: Speech, Chant and Song in an Appalachian Baptist Church.* Austin: University of Texas Press, 1988.

Torrance. Alan J. *Persons in Communion: Trinitarian Description and Human Participation.* Edinburgh: T. and T. Clark, 1996.

Torrance, Thomas F. *The Trinitarian Faith: An Evangelical Theology of the Ancient Catholic Church.* Edinburgh: T. and T. Clark, 1988.

Tracy, David. *Plurality and Ambiguity: Hermeneutics, Religion, Hope.* San Francisco: Harper and Row, 1987.

——. *The Analogical Imagination: Christian Theology and the Culture of Pluralism.* New York: Crossroad, 1981.

——. *Blessed Rage for Order: The New Pluralism in Theology.* New York: Crossroad, 1978.

Troeltsch, Ernst. *The Social Teaching of the Christian Churches.* Ed. H. Richard Niebuhr. Tr. Olive Wyon. New York: Harper, 1960.

Weber, Max. *The Sociology of Religion.* Tr. Ephraim Fischoff. Boston: Beacon Press, 1963.

Westermann, Claus. *What Does the Old Testament Say about God?* Sprunt Lectures for 1977, Union Seminary in Virginia, Richmond, Va. Atlanta: John Knox Press, 1979.

Wind, James P. *Places of Worship.* Nashville: American Association for State and Local History, 1990.

Wind, James P., and James W. Lewis, eds. *American Congregations*. Vol. 1. *Portraits of Twelve Religious Communities*. Chicago: University of Chicago Press, 1994.

Witten, Marsha G. *All Is Forgiven: The Secular Message in American Protestantism*. Princeton: Princeton University Press, 1993.

Wittgenstein, Ludwig. *Culture and Value*. Ed. G. H. von Wright and Heikki Nyman. Tr. Peter Winch. Chicago: University of Chicago Press, 1980.

Wood, Charles. *The Formation of Christian Understanding: Theological Hermeneutics*. 2nd ed. Valley Forge: Trinity Press International, 1993.

Zenger, Erich. *A God of Vengeance? Understanding the Psalms of Divine Wrath*. Tr. Linda M. Maloney. Louisville: Westminster/John Knox Press, 1994.

Zizioulas, John. *Being as Communion: Studies in Personhood and the Church*. Crestwood, N.Y.: St. Vladimir's Seminary Press, 1997.

Articles, Papers, and Parts of Books

Bellah, Robert N. "Is There a Common American Culture?" Address to the American Academy of Religion. San Francisco, November 22, 1997.

Bellah, Robert N., Richard Madsen, William M. Sullivan, Ann Swindler, and Steven Tipton. "Individualism and the Crisis of Civic Membership." *Christian Century*, May 8, 1996.

Campbell, Charles L. "Principalities, Powers and Preaching: Learning from William Stringfellow." *Interpretation* 51 (October 1997), no. 4.

Rebecca Chopp. Unpublished response to Walter Brueggemann's paper, "Texts That Linger, Words That Explode." American Academy of Religion/Society for Biblical Literature. Frontiers in Biblical Scholarship: The Endowmen for Biblical Lecture Series. Philadelphia. November 19, 1995.

"Disappearing Church." *Christian Century*, March 18–25, 1992.

Ferguson, John. "Courting Teamwork." *Life and Work*, February 1996.

Frank, Thomas E. "Ecclesial Vision and the Realities of Congregational Life." *Quarterly Review*, Spring 1992.

Gibson, Ivor. "Recovering Belief." *Life and Work*, January 1996.

Hall, Douglas John. "An Awkward Church." Theology and Worship Occasional Paper no. 5. Louisville: Presbyterian Church (U.S.A.), n.d.

———. "Remembered Voices, Neglected Words: The Unclaimed Legacy of 'Neo-Orthodoxy.'" Thomas White Currie Lectures. Austin Presbyterian Theological Seminary, January 29–31, 1996.

Hamilton, George. Untitled article. *Life and Work*, May 1995.

Hill, Robin. "Strolling to the Precipice." *Life and Work*, January 1996.

———. "Another Slice, Minister?" *Life and Work*, May 1995.

Jinkins, Michael. "The 'True Remedy': Jonathan Edwards' Soteriological Perspective As Observed in His Revival Treatises." *Scottish Journal of Theology* 48 (1995), no. 2.

———. "'The Being of Beings': Jonathan Edwards' Understanding of God As Reflected in His Final Treatises." *Scottish Journal of Theology* 46 (1993), no. 2.

———. "John Cotton and the Antinomian Controversy, 1636–1638: A Profile of Experiential Individualism in American Puritanism." *Scottish Journal of Theology* 43 (1990), no. 3.

Jinkins, Michael, and Stephen Breck Reid. "John McLeod Campbell on Christ's Cry of Dereliction: A Case Study in Trinitarian Hermeneutics." *EQ: The Evangelical Quarterly* 70 (1998), no. 2.

————. "God's Godforsakenness: The Cry of Dereliction As an Utterance within the Trinity," *Horizons in Biblical Theology: An International Dialogue* 19 (June 1997), no. 1.

Johnson, Luke Timothy. "Debate and Discernment: Scripture and the Spirit." *Commonweal*, January 28, 1994.

Longmuir, Bill. "Forward Planning Pays Off." *Life and Work*, September 1995.

McEvoy, J. P. "Is Hawking Another Albert Einstein?" *Times* (London), October 23, 1995.

"Methodism Slated To Disappear in Britain?" *Christian Century*, May 8, 1996.

Office of the General Assembly of the Presbyterian Church (U.S.A.), Minutes, 208th General Assembly, January 1–December 31, 1996, part 2.

Paton, Iain. "A Sign of Vitality." *Life and Work*, September 1994.

Perkins, Pheme. "The Gospel of Mark." In *The New Interpreter's Bible Commentary*. Vol. 8. Nashville: Abingdon Press, 1995.

"Problems Plague UMC's Study of Problems." *Christian Century*, February 29, 1994.

Rigby, Cynthia. "Free to be Human: Limits, Possibilities, and the Sovereignty of God." *Theology Today* 53 (April 1996), no. 1.

Segal, Robert A. "The 'De-Sociologizing' of the Sociology of Religion." *Scottish Journal of Religious Studies* 8 (Spring 1986), no. 1.

Smith, Julie. "Get Relevant." *Life and Work*, March 1996.

Storrar, William. "The Decline of the Kirk." *University of Aberdeen Divinity Alumni Association Newsletter*, Autumn 1997.

Stroup, George W. "A Lover's Quarrel: Theology and the Church." In *The Seminary: A School of the Church: Speeches from the Presidential Inauguration*. Austin: Austin Presbyterian Theological Seminary, November 14, 1997.

Tertullian. "The Martyrdom of Perpetua and Felicitas." In vol. 3 of *The Ante-Nicene Fathers*, ed. Alexander Roberts and James Donaldson (Grand Rapids: Eerdmans, 1980).

Torrance, Iain. "Between Legalism and Liberalism: Wisdom in Christian Ethics." In *But Where Shall Wisdom Be Found*, ed. Alan Main. Aberdeen: Aberdeen University Press, 1995.

"United Methodists Show Age, Says Survey." *Christian Century*, July 5–12, 1995.

Untitled article. *Christian Century*, August 12–19, 1992.

Untitled article. *Life and Work*, May 1995.

Untitled article. *Life and Work*, May 1995.

Van Marter, Jerry. "Daily Summary" of the General Assembly of the Presbyterian Church (U.S.A.) June 19, 1996. www.pcusa.org

Woodward, Kenneth L. "Dead End for the Mainline?" *Newsweek*, August 9, 1993.

Index